Gifted Children and Legal Issues in Education: Parents' Stories of Hope

Frances A. Karnes, Ph.D.
and
Ronald G. Marquardt, Ph.D., J.D.

KF
4209.5
.G54
1991
apr./1998

Published by Ohio Psychology Press, P.O. Box 90095,
Dayton, Ohio 45490. Copyright © 1991

Library of Congress Cataloging-in-Publication Data

Gifted children and legal issues in education: parents' stories of
hope / [edited by] Frances A. Karnes and Ronald G. Marquardt.
    p.   cm.
Includes bibliographical references and index.
ISBN 0-910707-16-2: $15.00
    1. Gifted children — Education — Law and legislation —
United States.
    2. Gifted children — Legal status, laws, etc. — United States.
I. Karnes, Frances A. II. Marquardt, Ronald G., 1939-   .
KF4209.5.G54   1991
334.73'07915 — dc20
[347.3047915]
                                                    91-21557
                                                    CIP

DEDICATED TO OUR CHILDREN
AND THE NEXT GENERATION.

Acknowledgements

We wish to thank the parents who took the time to relate and document their experiences. For some contributors, this involved a painful recounting of a frustrating period in the family history. These parents have shared the sorrows and joys of their experiences so that others with gifted children will know they are not alone as they seek the very best education for the sons and daughters with whom they have been blessed. These parents offer hope to all who desire and pursue excellence in education.

We trust that these stories, individually and collectively, will be of benefit and lend encouragement to other parents as they seek solutions to problems and attempt to eliminate roadblocks which impede the educational progress of their gifted and talented children.

Table of Contents

Foreword

*Gifted Children and Legal Issues in Education: Parents'
Stories of Hope* is a moving set of reports on the trials and
tribulations of parents who strive for an appropriate and high
quality education for their gifted and talented children. Their
struggles with the legal aspects and obstacles of the system
are vividly recounted in these thirteen stories. The stories
are presented as written by parents. After an introduction
which sets the stage by offering the basic information which
all advocates of the gifted should have, the book offers one
set of stories on early admission and the general problem of
admission to programs, a second set on parents' efforts to
get proper instruction for their gifted children, and a third
set on early high school graduation and the awarding of credits. An excellent appendix closes the book with lists of
contacts and information sources, a model constitution for
a parent association, and guidelines for parents and teachers
of the gifted.

A companion volume exists which is also a major contribution to the literature in the field of gifted education and
the law, and which should be read along with the present
book. This companion volume is entitled *Gifted Children
and the Law: Mediation, Due Process and Court Cases.*
After many years of sporadic exposure in magazines, newspapers, and occasionally in professional journals to court
cases involving gifted or talented youth and their families,
we finally have a well organized and carefully interpreted
compendium of all the major legal foci and issues related to
the education of gifted and talented youth. Frances A. Karnes
and Ronald G. Marquardt took a highly technical subject
matter and rendered it in clear, readable and truly interesting
fashion. The authors review natural law, constitutional law,
statutory law, administrative law, common law, and equity

law and the court structure in America. They also review the legal aspects of gifted education and due process state by state in comprehensive detail. Finally the appendix of the book is a rich source of information for parents and professional advocates of gifted education on sources of help, appropriate contact agencies, and professional contacts.

Gifted Children and Legal Issues in Education: Parents' Stories of Hope is the affective message favored by advocates of the gifted and talented. It touches the heart in its presentation of the struggles faced by gifted children and their parents in their endeavors to get a decent education. These two volumes will have a profound impact on the field of gifted education. They are must reading for *all* professionals in gifted education, and parents will find them a rich source of information and guidance as they go about the task of educating teachers, administrators, and school boards about the needs of gifted students and the special services they need to fulfill their potential to become creative productive leaders in our society.

John F. Feldhusen, Ph.D.
Purdue University

Preface

This collection of personal stories is based on actual experiences of parents of gifted children. These parents made concerted efforts to overcome or bypass various obstacles so that their gifted elementary and secondary children could gain access to challenging educational programs appropriate to their unique needs. In some cases, groups of parents launched campaigns to get school boards and administrators to initiate and provide programs and services for the gifted in accordance with existing school statutes. In other cases, parents worked to obtain provisions for appropriate education through less conventional means.

The stories appear as written by the parents who submitted them, except for minimal editing which was done without making substantive changes. We tried to preserve the writing style and language parents used to describe their experiences in seeking the most promising educational opportunities for their gifted sons and daughters. All families have chosen to reveal their identities, except one. Those parents wish to remain anonymous.

The parents who submitted these stories are representative of many parents of the nation in that their standards of living range from moderate to the high end of the socioeconomic continuum. These parents range in age from young to mid-life and beyond, and represent various ethnic groups. The children who are central in these stories ranged from preschool to the senior year in secondary school when these events took place. They lived in different sections of the country, and their home and school settings range from rural to intermediate urban to large city environments. Typically, the family unit includes two or more children. Most of the stories were written by the parents within the last eighteen months, from late 1989 through early 1991.

While the children described in these stories all have characteristics that justify their classification as gifted, they do vary in their abilities and in the means by which they were identified or recognized as being gifted. Some children with very high scores on intelligence tests are considered intellectually gifted, while those who do exceptionally well on achievement tests are recognized as being academically talented. Parents hope, of course, that all gifted children will fulfill the parents' expectations and achieve to their full potential. Some of the youth may possess abilities and attributes that enable them to excel in the areas of creativity, leadership, and the fine and performing arts, but these were not the reasons for seeking solutions to problems and conflicts which arose. Instead, students in the following stories faced difficulties because of their academic and intellectual abilities.

Each story is unique, but collectively certain patterns emerge. Typically, the parents who sought recourse when confronted with obstacles which stood between their children and a quality education, did so in the interest of the total educational experience of their children rather than one specialized phase of the educational enterprise. Facing real obstacles in the path of progress for their children, or coming to an impasse when confronted with school policies, regulations, or decisions which seemed to mitigate against optimum educational opportunities for their sons and daughters, these parents of gifted children stood firm and took appropriate action.

This book is divided into an introduction and three subsequent sections. The introduction provides information that every parent and advocate of a gifted child should know. The parent perspectives in Part I describe early admission to school and situations involving admissions to gifted programs. Part II relates the efforts of parents to secure appropriate placement and instruction for their children. The awarding of Carnegie Units and early graduation from high school are the themes of the stories in Part III.

In some cases, the problems were relatively easy to solve. However, some parents were faced with situations which, after investing a great deal of time and effort, they perceived to be hopeless. In desperation, they sold their homes and moved to a new school district which offered more promising educational opportunities for their children. Several of the parents achieved their goals by making effective use of due process hearings, while other found it advisable to seek recourse in the courts. In all cases, the lack, or inaccessibility, of appropriate educational opportunities for the gifted has been a source of anxiety and frustration for the families, and for some, this has entailed a heavy financial burden as well. In some situations, local school personnel and state educational staff could have been better informed and more cooperative, while in other instances these professionals were very helpful as they came forward with mutually acceptable solutions.

We wish to thank the parents who took the time to relate and document their experiences. For some contributors, this involved a painful recounting of a frustrating period in the family history. These parents have shared the sorrows and joys of their experiences so that others with gifted children will know they're not alone as they seek the very best education for the sons and daughters with whom they have been blessed. These parents offer hope to all who desire and pursue excellence in education.

We trust that these stories, individually and collectively, will be of benefit and lend encouragement to other parents as they seek solutions to problems and attempt to eliminate roadblocks which impede the educational progress of their gifted and talented children. There are individual states with laws which make it mandatory that free and appropriate public education be provided to all gifted children and have policies and procedures directed to that goal. However, until the importance of taking such steps is fully recognized and accepted nationally, and until there are federal and state mandates which provide clear safeguards for the educational rights of the gifted and talented throughout the land, parents and other advocates must continue to do all they can to open the doors to free and appropriate public education for these children.

Several sources of information on gifted education are provided in Suggested Readings and in the Appendices. The names and addresses of the state consultants appear in Appendix A. National and international groups in gifted education are listed in Appendix B. Journals and magazines focusing on the gifted appear in Appendix C. For parents and other concerned adults who wish to form an advocacy group, a sample constitution is given in Appendix D. Ideas on bridging the gap in communication between home and school are provided in Appendix E. A bibliography is provided for additional sources of the useful information.

These stories are presented from the perspective of parents who take very seriously their obligation to do all they can to promote the interests of their gifted children and their education. They do not represent the reflections of the school personnel or others mentioned in the stories. School administrators have alternative means of communication such as professional textbooks, journals, and conferences to relate their viewpoints. This book presents a unique outlet for parents to express their concerns to other parents, teachers, and school officials.

We hope to revise this volume on a regular basis by presenting additional information about the progress made by the children who are the central subjects in these stories, and by adding reports on the more recent experiences of other parents who seek excellence in the education of their gifted children. Parents who wish to share their struggles are invited to contact the authors by mail addressed to:

Dr. Frances A. Karnes/Dr. Ronald G. Marquardt
Institute for Law and Gifted Education
909 South 34th Avenue
Hattiesburg, MS 39402

Introduction

Before proceeding to the parents' stories, a few initial remarks seem in order. These comments are based on our experiences in counseling parents who faced problems obtaining an appropriate education for their gifted children. Many of these ideas were also gleaned from the literature in gifted education and legal references. You will recognize these points as you read the parents' success stories.

We recently completed a companion volume, *Gifted Children and the Law: Mediation, Due Process and Court Cases.* (Karnes & Marquardt, 1991). Our thesis is that parents should avoid the courts in settling disputes in gifted education, if at all possible. There are several good reasons for this advice, but perhaps the strongest is that the time, effort, and resources required to fight a court battle could best be spent on educational matters. Many parents are unpleasantly surprised at how quickly legal fees soar when a dispute heads for the courts. Two sets of parents told us they had spent the same amount, $20,000, in legal costs without obtaining a resolution of the problem. Along these lines, *Gifted Children and the Law: Mediation, Due Process and Court Cases* devotes several chapters to ways of solving gifted education concerns without going to court. However, as one exasperated parent yelled from the back of a meeting room where we were speaking at a national conference, "Sometimes you just have to go to court." Indeed you do, and *Gifted Children and the Law: Mediation, Due Process and Court Cases* includes three chapters discussing many of the seminal cases already decided in gifted education. In several of the stories in this volume, parents ended their struggle with a courtroom victory. Generally speaking, however, it is best to solve a dispute within the school system, before reaching the courts.

While there is no one best strategy to settle a dispute in gifted education, there are several steps parents and educators can take to reduce the time and money required to solve a problem. The first goal should be to solve the dispute at the lowest possible rung in the administrative ladder. Many problems can be solved by the classroom teacher; if not, you may be able to enlist the classroom teacher as an ally. If you are certain that the matter requires the attention of persons higher in the administrative hierarchy, again start with the school official closest to the problem and work your way up the ladder. This short-circuits the "bureaucratic shuffle" where disgruntled parents are sent back to the building principal or supervisor of gifted education. If you are going to be shuffled, you want to be sent up the administrative ladder rather than down. You can then assure the person who has the decision-making power that you have sought help from all of his or her subordinates and you are ready to seriously negotiate.

While you are working your way through the administrative maze, take the following steps to facilitate the resolution of your dispute.

1. Secure and carefully read the written policies and procedures on gifted education from the local school district.
2. Beginning with the first telephone call or visit to the school, keep a diary of your efforts. You may think you will remember the substance of a conversation you had with a teacher or school official on a certain day, but the details may fade with time.
3. After each visit, summarize the discussion in a letter. This will also serve as a record of the conversation for you and the school official. Remember, some of these disputes will last for months or even years. One of the seminal court cases in gifted education lasted six years from inception to the final decision by the Pennsylvania Supreme Court.

4. Discuss your situation with others. Your first reaction when a problem arises may be to think that it's you against the world. You may feel, as comedian George Gobel put it, "like a brown shoe in a world of tuxedos." But in all probability other parents may be experiencing the same concerns regarding gifted education in a particular school district or state.

5. As discussed in the story "Sixteen Heads Are Better Than One," collective actions are often productive. You avoid being designated as a discontented individual, and you have other parents with whom you can exchange ideas and receive support. Parents may wish to form an interest group to articulate gifted education goals for their school district. A sample constitution for a community gifted education association is found in Appendix D.

6. When attempting to secure information on other situations involving legal matters in gifted education, don't be discouraged when such information is not readily available. Due process hearings are on occasion closed; state education officials are often reluctant to release the results, especially in a personally identifiable manner. Court records involving juveniles are often sealed and inaccessible to the public. Some situations, of course, are settled before trial and the settlement terms are known only to the participants, who are sometimes pledged to secrecy. In the few cases where a dispute matures into an open trial, it is only if, and when, the cases are appealed to the appellate courts that they appear in law case books. But while the information may be difficult to obtain, procedures do exist to secure the necessary information in most situations. The stories in this book provide model strategies which may be adapted to other circumstances.

7. Remember that national gifted education associations can also be of help (see Appendix B). State personnel in gifted education will provide helpful advice and materials as well (see Appendix A). Don't be afraid to tap the insights of these professionals who can provide assistance based upon years of experience in the field of gifted education. They are just a telephone call or a letter away, and you may benefit from being forced to define the issues of your dispute in your communication with these gifted education advocates. State consultants in gifted education can provide the names and addresses of persons in leadership positions in local and state associations. Several general publications relating to gifted education advocacy are listed at the end of this book (see Appendix C).

8. Sometime during the working out of the solution to the dispute, it is wise to step back and let others evaluate the specifics of your problem. We all want the best for our children and we all take great pride in their abilities and accomplishments. However, sometimes this parental pride can be blinding. Get an impartial second opinion as to what is in the best interest of your child. Perhaps he or she should remain in the same grade, or not be bused to a gifted program across town, or stay at the same reading level as most of his or her peers. Receiving a second opinion from a university specialist in gifted education, a private psychologist, or an independent testing group can force you to rethink your goals; or, if the experts' views are congruent with what you believe to be the best interest of your child, it can reinforce your aspirations. Either way, your situation is improved by seeking a second opinion.

9. After discussion with appropriate officials, if the decision is to go forward with negotiations with the school

district, you then must take the next step and arm your-self with the relevant state statutes and administrative regulations pertaining to your situation. This may take some effort, but you must know what the law and policies and procedures are concerning the facet of gifted education involved in the dispute. The school administrators will have a board attorney to advise them; make certain you are on an even playing field by knowing the relevant law. Again, associations for gifted education, university professors, and others can be of help. Many times the laws are spread throughout the statute books and regulations promulgated by the state education department. Seek help in finding the relevant law and don't be satisfied with a guess as to what the law is on a particular issue. Most school administrators work on a daily basis with school law and are usually competent in the area. To negotiate successfully, you need an equal degree of knowledge regarding what the law is concerning gifted education and related areas in your particular state. Secure the laws and rules and regulations in writing. Do not rely on hearsay for this vital information.

10. Knowing the relevant law and rules and regulations also means being informed as to what procedures are available in your state to obtain relief. States vary as to procedures available to parents. Some states offer mediation, an opportunity for a due process hearing before an impartial hearing officer, administrative review of the state education department, and then an opportunity to be heard in the courts. In many states, judges will insist that the administrative remedies be tried before they will hear the lawsuit. As discussed earlier, in most instances it will be to your advantage to solve the dispute at the lowest level. Again, the associations listed in the appendices will be able to aid you in getting

information on the informal remedies available in your state.

Going to Court

Should your only choice be a resolution in court, proceed with caution. Be very careful when selecting an attorney. Most lawyers do not practice education law. It is not in the required curriculum of law schools; education suits are not the standard fare of most lawyers. Therefore, the attorney who handled your automobile accident claim is probably not the best one for you in a dispute in gifted education. Inquire as to your prospective attorney's experience with education law; if you need help finding a knowledgeable lawyer, check with your state bar association or the associations listed at the end of this book. It is unethical under the canons of attorney ethics for a lawyer to take a case in a field where he or she has no expertise. Remember that it is your money and your child's future that is at stake. Both are too precious to waste on an incompetent attorney.

Once you find a knowledgeable attorney, determine how the fees will be charged to your account. Some attorneys feel it is unprofessional or awkward to discuss money but you need to know an approximate figure. In some instances it may be difficult to estimate what the total cost will be, but you should know if fees will be charged monthly, at the end of the case, etc. Unless you can place your case in some kind of civil rights category, in most states there is no fee shifting statute which awards fees to prevailing plaintiffs in cases in gifted education. That is, each side pays its own attorney fees no matter how the case is decided. Because the school district has legal counsel available whose services are paid by the taxpayers of the district, unless you are wealthy, the advantage in securing legal services clearly rests with the school district. Therefore, you must marshall your legal resources wisely. For example, if the issue warrants it, a class action case where several parties sue the district in a single suit would allow the plaintiffs to share the legal expenses involved in the suit. Or, perhaps a gifted association will provide legal support by providing assistance to your attorney or by filing an *amicus curiae* (friend of the court) brief in an appellate case.

Surviving the Conflict

Finally, one other point. Parents who develop an adversarial relationship with a school district often find themselves shouldering a heavy burden. For many persons the school district is sacrosanct and parents who challenge school policies often face threats and property damage. Parents have related their feelings of being ostracized by the community and often the community's contempt has taken the form of egg throwing, public ridicule, etc. In one case, the plaintiffs surmised they lost their case simply because the jurors preferred not to risk injuring the school district in any way. If the jury held the school district at fault, the unsuccessful plaintiffs concluded, the jury believed there would be a negative reflection on the community. And because the jurors were part of the community, that meant a negative reflection on the jurors themselves.

Adults can survive such periods of strife. Children, however, who are the subject of the disputes, must be protected. Administrators, teachers, and parents must be vigilant that disputes do not carry into the classroom and affect the student's academic performance or social-emotional development. If parents believe that such developments are taking place, a conference with appropriate school personnel should be scheduled immediately. Parents also need to be sensitive to the fact that disputes can "spill over" and affect school personnel attitudes toward other children in the family.

On a positive note, what follows is a group of stories written by parents who have successfully settled a dispute for an educational opportunity for their children. The stories are inspirational and provide hope for gifted education advocates throughout America. More important, they are accounts of struggles which reflect the best of the American experience — winning a battle to protect a minority. And similar to the battles that have been fought to win opportunities for other minorities, all of society benefits when children are allowed to reach their full potential.

Part I

Admission to Schools and Programs

The White Family

The White family lives in Petal, Mississippi, and includes Adriana, age thirteen, who is presently enrolled in the ninth grade, Andrew, age eleven, who is in the seventh grade, and Alexis, age five, who will be enrolled in the first grade. Glenn White received a B.A. degree in Political Science from the University of Southern Mississippi. He subsequently enrolled in the University of Mississippi Law School and received a J.D. degree in 1977. The mother, Robin, left high school during her junior year to enroll at the University of Southern Mississippi in their early admittance program. Although she completed approximately three years toward a nursing degree, her education was interrupted due to the birth of their daughter. Subsequently, she completed her studies at the University and received a B.S. in Psychology with a minor in Criminal Justice. Glenn is presently employed as the District Attorney for the Twelfth Judicial District, and Robin works as a Forrest County Victim/Witness Coordinator.

Just Because It's the Law,
It Isn't Necessarily So

When my eldest daughter was about three years old, we enrolled her in an early education center under the auspices of an education department at a local college. It was our intention to provide her with a learning opportunity and not just a day care facility. We also felt it would be beneficial for her to have social opportunities with other children her age.

Tests administered when Adriana was four years and four months of age revealed that her IQ was above normal and that she had a mental age approximating that of a seven-year-old child. The following year, test results indicated that she could perform mathematics on approximately a third grade level. Her grasp of general information approached that of a second grader. In addition, she could read and spell. With these results, we were confident that she could perform school work, even though her birth date was three months past the arbitrary cutoff day for enrollment in public schools. We were advised by educational personnel that the program she had enrolled in for the past two years would not challenge her and the material would be repetitive. As a result, we considered the possibility of enrolling her in public school but were faced with the birth date disqualification. We explored the possibility of enrolling her in a private school with the eventual transfer back into the public sector. While we were exploring this opportunity, several people in the education field indicated that we should just allow her to have a break and enroll her in a play school. Others advised us that it would make absolutely no difference and she would be on the same level with other students by the time she reached the third grade.

After several phone calls, I made a personal appearance before the superintendent of education, members of the school board, and school board attorney concerning the possibility of allowing her to enroll even though the law indicated otherwise. I provided the school board with the results of the tests. Further, I had letters indicating that she was both mentally and emotionally mature enough to perform satisfactorily on the first grade level. The board took the position that the law did not allow for any exemption, and they did not have the authority to allow her to enroll. As I had perceived the position of the school board, the only barrier to her enrollment was her chronological age. As a result, I then explored, with the attorney for the school board, the possibility of filing a lawsuit.

I eventually filed the lawsuit in state court, attaching and making a record of all the tests that had been accomplished, as well as statements and affidavits indicating that she was mentally and emotionally mature enough to enroll. We charged that she was being denied her due process of law and the right to a public education through rigid adherence to a requirement which discriminated against her solely because of her age. Since the school board did not dispute the fact that she was capable of performing satisfactorily in first grade, the facts themselves were not in dispute in court. The only issue which the school board addressed in their answer was that they were precluded from admitting her based upon a state statute which did not allow an exemption.

After the judge reviewed the documents that were submitted, he filed an order authorizing the school board to accept her admission and ordered that she be allowed to enroll. My daughter performed in an exemplary manner and was actually placed in an accelerated class. She is presently in accelerated eighth grade classes and is enrolled in gifted studies. Despite the predictions to the contrary, there was no evidence of her abilities being diminished at third grade — to the contrary, she seemed to excel even further.

We also have a son who is two years younger than our daughter. His birthday fell one month after the cutoff date for enrollment in school. As a result of our pleasant experiences in placing Adriana in an early learning environment, we again looked at the possibility, after Andrew had completed two years of preschool, of enrolling him in the public school program. I followed the same procedure again and was successful in obtaining a court order authorizing his enrollment in school. There have been absolutely no problems with his early enrollment.

My wife and I are strong advocates of early educational opportunities for three- and four-year-old children who have demonstrated the aptitude and maturity to succeed in school. We have been very successful in locating those services in our area and have been able to obtain early enrollment for our children. It was amazing for us to see how much knowledge they could absorb at such an early age.

If a parent is faced with the same situation as we were, time and prior planning are of the utmost importance. It took us approximately nine months of planning to be able to successfully enroll Adriana in school. My advice to parents who have a five-year-old that they feel should be granted early admission to the public schools would be to begin planning immediately. Gather all data, such as test scores and letters from teachers, which attest to the child's ability, and provide that information to the appropriate school board. In the event that you are unsuccessful in convincing the school board to allow an early enrollment, I would talk to the school board attorney about filing a lawsuit to get a court order authorizing early enrollment. Again, I would reiterate that prior planning must be done in order to accomplish this. Parents must allow for the time it takes to obtain documents, as well as the delays that occur in filing a lawsuit, if this becomes necessary.

Although all parents feel that their children are special, it is imperative, if parents are considering the possibility of enrolling their child in public schools at an earlier age, that they gather documentation to objectively establish, through independent means, the ability of the child or children to perform academically. Even with this kind of evidence, it is a struggle, but we obviously believe the time and effort spent results in educational dividends. After all, we repeated the experience three times.

The Davis Family

The Davis family lives on a farm near Worden, Illinois. Steve Davis is a full-time elementary school teacher, He also has a tax business, and spends much of every spring planting crops for three hundred acres. His wife, Mary Jane Davis, has her hands full teaching full-time, raising a family, and fulfilling her many farm obligations.

Mary Jane has a bachelor's degree from Valley City University in North Dakota. She is currently a kindergarten teacher. Steve has a bachelor's degree in education from the University of Evansville in Indiana. He has a master's degree in school administration from the University of Missouri. He has also pursued additional hours of education at Webster University in Missouri, and Southern Illinois University at Edwardsville, Illinois. He is a computer specialist who teaches students from first through sixth grades in the school's computer learning center.

Mary Jane and Steve are the parents of Sam Henry, Katie, and Stephen James Jr. Sam Henry is fifteen and a sophomore at Staunton High School. He is active in Boy Scouts and is currently working on his Eagle project. Last year he attended the National Jamboree in Virginia. Katie is twelve and in sixth grade. She is a busy girl who plays the piano and saxophone, enjoys school dramatic activities, and loves to spend as much time as possible with her horse. She received the Presidential Academic Fitness Award this year. Stephen Jr. just turned ten in May and is in fourth grade at Staunton. He is excited about Cub Scouts, fishing and mini-bikes.

Since the school district detachment proceeding has been resolved in their favor, the Davis family has built a new home on their farm and are happy exactly where they are.

No Gifted Program?
Try Legally Moving the Family Farm

· ·My wife and I, both being educators, realized that the Worden, Illinois School District was inadequate, mostly due to a lack of tax base and subsequent funding. We had discussed selling the farm, which would have been an easier proposition had we only been discussing a house. We considered putting a trailer a half mile down the road in the Staunton School District. Also, we talked of private schools and finally, in the spring of 1983, we began the series of events which led to the annexation of our farm to another school district and to a final mandate by the Illinois Appellate Court in June of 1987. In the fall of 1983, Sam and Katie would be starting fourth grade and kindergarten, whereas, Steve Jr. would only be three years old.

In the spring of 1983, at the urging of other parents who felt the inadequacy of the Worden Schools, we scheduled a meeting for those interested in consolidation. However, a lot of people came who opposed consolidation. They told us that we had only lived there ten years and we had no right to discuss consolidation. They said that they would block the change no matter what. One person stated they would sell popcorn on the streets to fund the schools. Needless to say, nothing came of the meeting other than an emotional debate.

In the fall of 1983, our children were placed in a Lutheran School even though we did not belong to that church. Aside from the improved school situation, a fight with the school district warranted this change for several reasons. One was legal/financial in terms of removing any state reimbursement for our children to Worden. Another was common sense: to remove our children from an environment where it would be natural for negative feelings to be harbored.

Next we went to see an attorney who had just won an educational law case for three of our neighbors. Itappeared he was taking our case, but after about a month he canceled. We have some idea why, but it is speculation on our part. Next, on the advice of someone, and we are not sure who, my wife made an appearance at the Worden School Board meeting to encourage consolidation and the response was that the school system was adequate.

Finally, in January of 1984, we retained an attorney we knew through our teacher's union. He had been a teacher and handled many cases for the Illinois Federation of Teachers. Certainly he was no stranger to Illinois school law. This attorney prepared the detachment papers, and the hearing before the county (regional) school board was conducted on April 23, 1984. The transcript of the total hearing is available from the regional superintendent's office; however, it is lengthy.

Here are some of the highlights of the case we presented. On curriculum comparison we showed Staunton schools to have an agricultural program, a gifted program, home economics, shop, computers, art, music, foreign language, extracurricular plays, band, football, baseball and golf, etc. None of these could be found in the Worden Schools. Also, the mathematics, English, and science programs were at a bare minimum in Worden, while much more was being offered in these subject areas in Staunton. Worden had no vocational program available but did provide a one-hour bus ride each way to another district. The program in the Staunton District was adequate and on campus. We realized, after observation and examination of test results, that a gifted program was important since Katie's IQ appeared to be above 140. We were certain her IQ was above normal, at the same time realizing that it had not yet stabilized. Sam was interested in the farm, and we pointed to the agricultural program as being important.

The county school board consisted of seven members. We knew the backgrounds of four of the members. The president of the board was a practicing attorney. One board member was a surveyor. Another member was a retired school superintendent, and one was a farmer.

The county school board voted against us, five to two, and by that action, disallowed our detachment from Worden District to Staunton. The two minority votes came from the retired school superintendent and the attorney, whom we think are the only persons on the board who have earned college degrees. The retired school superintendent stated that, because of the merit of the educational case we presented for our children, his vote would have to be with us. The attorney, who was Board President, spoke last and pleaded with the other board members to reconsider, because the facts were with us as we had met all five points of law and the courts would likely reverse the decision of the county board not to allow detachment. At this point one of the other members commented that he would like to see us take it to court; it only costs money. The reasons given for opposing us were shallow and included protecting the tax base, helping the economy of the county, and keeping the school district of Worden from being irreparably damaged with a .3 percent income loss.

After the session, a board member approached us to say it didn't matter what kind of school your kids went to if they wanted to learn. We countered that it is terribly hard to learn a foreign language or receive special help as a gifted student if there is no program in place to offer these opportunities. That same board member told us that agricultural courses were not that important and all that's needed to be a farmer is to take a welding course.

We lost round one, as our attorney said we would if the board let their emotions overrule the facts. We filed an appeal with the circuit court in May 1984, received a hearing in January 1986, and obtained a reversal of the regional board's decision on April 1, 1986.

The board appealed to the Illinois Appellate Court in April 1986, and a mandate upholding the lower court's reversal of the regional board's decision was upheld. As our attorney stated, the war was finally over. This process took us four years and two months.

Obviously, we were very satisfied. The greatest hurdle was the amount of time, effort, and money that had to be expended for something as simple as this situation. Certainly we would fight the battle again. Our advice to others in our position is to start early, get an outstanding attorney who is well versed in school law, and possibly seek some help from an educator on curriculum comparisons.

A couple of final comments. It's sad to think that many parents of gifted children or of children interested in a special program, whether it be agriculture, computers, or whatever, would not be able to carry on this kind of fight financially. We are not wealthy. We both need to work, and the expense was tough but worth it, since we give education the highest priority. We would have been willing to work within the Worden School System, had we thought there was anything to work with or any hope of providing an adequate program for students.

Because of an inadequate program and mounting debt, Worden was to be annexed for the 1988–89 school year. State laws allowed only two choices: Worden could consolidate with Staunton (twelve miles closer for many residents) or Edwardsville. Both had good full programs, but the board chose to annex Worden into Edwardsville. Our opinion is that families like us caused a backlash against Staunton and the Worden Board made sure they went to Edwardsville. County politics may have also played a part in the decision.

For our part, we're glad our children went to Staunton. It's too bad others who want to go to Staunton can't do so without transferring guardianship or some other legal circumvention of the law. It is also unfortunate that the Worden Board annexed by board decision rather than allowing citizens to vote, as could have been done.

Our detachment proceeding indicates the regional board of education did not understand that if they blatantly disregarded the facts, their decision could be overruled by the courts.

We hope our case will be a clear signal to school boards that poor educational judgment and irresponsible decision making are not acceptable.

The Cumberland Family

The Cumberland family, Luke, Susan, Annie, and Sara, live in Meridian, Mississippi, where the children attend Poplar Springs Elementary. Annie is eight and is in the third grade while Sara is six and is in kindergarten.

Luke has a bachelor's degree in social work and works as a regional supervisor with the Mississippi Division of Medicaid. Susan has a bachelor's degree in political science and has taken course work required for teacher certification in the following areas: kindergarten through eighth grade, secondary social studies, and gifted education. She was a full-time mother until both children entered school. Since Sara started kindergarten this year, she has worked as a substitute teacher.

No Gifted Program?
Change the Family Domicile

The year before our highly gifted daughter entered first grade, we learned that the Mississippi county school district that served our area did not offer programs for gifted students in the early grades. We also found that the city school district nearby did have programs for gifted students starting in the second grade. After discussion with both school districts, we were led to believe that our daughter would be able to transfer to the city school to take advantage of their special program. The city school personnel also indicated that there was a possibility that she could participate in the second grade gifted program while in the first grade. However, after school started and our daughter was enrolled in the city school, we were told that the two school districts had, during the summer, instituted a new policy which no longer allowed transfers between the districts.

We talked with the appropriate school personnel, assistant superintendent of the county schools and acting superintendent of the city schools, but were told that there was little likelihood that a transfer would be granted. The city school did agree to allow our daughter to remain in their school for a maximum of two months if we agreed to attempt to move so that we would be in the confines of their district. We also met with each member of the county school district's board and presented our case at their board meeting. After the county school board formally denied our request for the transfer, we appealed their decision to the State Department of Education. The State Department of Education overturned the school board's decision and granted the transfer.

While all this was happening, we began trying to sell our house and to purchase one in the city school district. We accomplished this around the first of November of that year and then resided in the proper district for our daughter to attend the school we felt was best for her.

Some time after this, the county school board appealed the decision of the State Board of Education that granted the transfer. The case was tried in the state capital, Jackson, Mississippi, and the Hinds County Chancery Judge ruled that the county school board had not acted improperly in denying our transfer request and overturned the decision of the State Board of Education. Of course, the whole issue was moot by this time since we had moved and were no longer affected by the decisions of the county school board.

At the very beginning of this process, we sought legal counsel. We found out that the transfer was going to be denied on a Friday afternoon and met with the attorney the next morning. But that attorney was not knowledgeable on laws affecting schools and his efforts on our behalf were not fruitful. We concluded that studying the laws regarding schools at our county legal library and handling this ourselves would be more productive.

After the county school board appealed the State Board of Education's decision to the Hinds County Chancery clerk, we again tried to find legal assistance in the preparation of our brief. We were still unable to find an attorney knowledgeable on school law who was willing to represent us. The only attorneys familiar with school law represented the school districts and were, therefore, unwilling to come in with someone on the other side. We finally prepared our brief by ourselves.

The attorney who first tried to help us contacted the school board members and the school board's attorney immediately after we talked with him. After we saw that his efforts were not helping, we met with the school board members and anyone else that we thought might be in a position to help us. All of this took place well before any legal proceedings.

Ultimately, our daughter wound up attending the school that we felt was best for her, and in that sense, we were satisfied. We were not pleased that we were forced to sell our house and move our family to accomplish this aim. We felt that the granting of a transfer by the county school district would have been the simplest and least disruptive means of providing appropriate educational opportunities for our daughter.

The almost universal lack of knowledge about, and understanding of, the special needs of the gifted students among educators was troubling. We were told by several of the county school board members that extra school work would suffice in meeting our daughter's needs. They did not seem to understand that gifted students need special programs with challenging, thought-provoking material. They were more concerned with adherence to their policy than with the needs of any individual student. The lack of any support group which had real power to influence the decision-making process also disturbed us.

The county school board's lack of knowledge about the special needs of the gifted and that the state did not, at that time, have provisions in school law which required an appropriate education for all children hindered our efforts. We were unable to convince school officials that our child did require special programs and that they had a responsibility to provide these programs if they were unwilling to grant a transfer to a school district which offered them.

There were several individuals and/or organizations that were helpful in our attempts to rectify our problems. Two university educators researching legal issues and the gifted offered much support and useful advice to us during this time. The officers of the Mississippi Association for the Talented and Gifted also provided moral support as well as suggestions that were very helpful.

We would definitely fight the battle again if a similar situation were to arise. Our daughter's education is very important to us and we feel that our efforts resulted in her receiving the opportunities she deserves. The city school system did place her in gifted programs while she was in first grade. Even though these programs are normally not available until the second grade, the officials of the school system recognized that she had special needs and worked with us to meet those needs. Since then, they have established a special program for highly gifted students in which our daughter has participated. This program offers an open-ended curriculum in which the students may advance as quickly as aptitude, effort, and achievement permit. School personnel have been open to our suggestions and desires regarding her education and have provided an appropriate and challenging curriculum for her. We do not believe that these opportunities and options would have been available if we had not taken the actions described above.

Persevere! We believe that parents must let the schools know that all children deserve an appropriate education and that we expect provision for it. If a parent does not think that an appropriate education is being provided by the school system, then it is the parent's right and responsibility to pursue all legal means to either change the system or find another system which will meet the child's needs. If the parent does not give up, the child will be able to obtain an appropriate education — which he or she needs in order to prosper and excel.

The Frana Family

Jerry and Linda Frana live in Grand Detour, Illinois. He received a B.S. in occupational education and she was awarded a B.A. in political science from Southern Illinois University. They have a keen interest in developing the educational talents of their one child, Jeremiah, who is ten. Linda presently is teaching Jeremiah in a home school situation and Jerry teaches in a local community college. When not pursuing excellence in education, the Franas enjoy music, reading, traveling, camping, swimming, gardening, photography and bike riding.

Home Schooling Was the Alternative to Retention

When Jeremiah was in kindergarten, we learned that the Challenge Program for gifted students was being developed in our district. The newspaper reported that testing for this program was being conducted for children who would be first graders in the fall. When we asked the kindergarten teacher at a parent/teacher conference if Jeremiah had been given such a test, her response was "no." Her explanation for denying Jeremiah this opportunity was "his behavior."

We felt that the Challenge classes would be appropriate placement for Jeremiah in first grade because of his many interests, his abilities, and his love of learning. In the spring of his kindergarten year, we requested the test for the Challenge Program be given to Jeremiah. This was not only for our own information, but also because we thought there might still be a chance for Jeremiah to enter the program in the fall. There are two tests in Jeremiah's kindergarten file, reading readiness and Otis-Lennon IQ. We are not sure if either test was required for determining eligibility for the program or if the test we requested was ever given. If any of these tests were used, Jeremiah would have met the academic criteria for the Challenge Program.

But it seems the most important criterion for entering the gifted program was teacher identification or recommendation. Without identification — and also because of an incorrectly scored Otis-Lennon test during the kindergarten year, which placed our son in the average IQ score range — Jeremiah was prevented from meeting any of the requirements. We didn't discover that the IQ test was incorrectly scored until near the end of the first grade.

When Jeremiah entered first grade, we saw problems and realized he was not being challenged in the regular class.

We suggested the idea of gifted programming as a possibility, and decided to have Jeremiah tested privately at our own expense. In the spring of Jeremiah's first grade year, we also wrote to the principal requesting a multidisciplinary conference. The school principal arranged a meeting of the counselor we had brought, the school psychologist, and other staff members. The school psychologist acknowledged that she had come to the meeting without knowing why she had been asked to attend. The psychologist had not seen the testing that we had done independently. Neither the social worker, nor the school psychologist, could understand what we wanted and why we were there. We presented to the principal some concerns about Jeremiah's not being "challenged" in school. It was apparent that the principal was not clear about the procedures for getting Jeremiah into the Challenge Program. Based on the principal's statement we assumed that Jeremiah could be bussed to the school that held the Challenge Program, a combined gifted class of first and second graders. He said this would be an ideal solution to Jeremiah's problem.

The school psychologist said she had not had a chance to read any of the testing and was only told that she needed to be at this meeting without being told why. The psychologist called a couple of days later and said that, after getting a chance to read the letter requesting the multidisciplinary conference, she wanted us to know that we hadn't received such a meeting. She would make arrangements to honor our request.

The multidisciplinary conference was held during the last week of Jeremiah's first grade year. We had spent much time, effort, and expense in obtaining professional evaluations and recommendations that might assist the school in assessing the present situation and determining appropriate planning for Jeremiah's educational future. We had even requested a

CAT scan and an EEG to determine whether any physical problems existed. The neurologist's report was available at this conference.

Other reports were available as well. We had one from an independent educational counseling service psychologist we had hired to share additional test results with the school system. Comments from the teacher of the learning disabilities (LD) classes at Jeremiah's school were available. She had also done some testing for the school for the multidisciplinary conference. Much later we learned that her written observations and opinions suggested that Jeremiah "is a gifted child in areas of reading, language, and spelling, but he does have selected learning disabilities in the areas of perceptual, visual, auditory, and fine motor." We later found that the LD resource specialist also had recommended that Jeremiah be "considered for placement in a gifted program in the aforementioned areas, with assistance in changing his behaviors to increase his ability to succeed in school." We did not know at the time of the conference that Jeremiah had been identified as gifted. Although the LD specialist was present, her comments were not mentioned at this conference. This is an important point, because one reason that we requested this multidisciplinary team meeting was to see if gifted services would be appropriate, after considering the testing the district had done and the added information we were providing.

As per our understanding, the Iowa Test of Basic Skills (at first grade level) along with teacher identification or recommendation were the means used to determine eligibility for our district's Challenge Program. The cutoff score for consideration for the gifted program was on the composite score of 80 percentile on the Iowa Test of Basic Skills. Jeremiah had a composite score of 79 percentile. There were several subtest scores at the 80 percentile or above on this test.

Thus, we felt it was worth the effort to go through this multidisciplinary process to see if Jeremiah would now be eligible for gifted services. We thought that he definitely needed the challenge and enrichment that a gifted program could provide.

We were under the impression, at the time, that the way to obtain services was through a multidisciplinary conference, which was a special education process. We were not aware that such a process was not also a means to receive "due process" for gifted as it was for special education. This multidisciplinary conference did not result in any services of any kind being recommended, either gifted or special education.

We requested several parent-school conferences during Jeremiah's third grade year. We brought a family counselor to at least two of these meetings with team members. We sought services from this counselor because Jeremiah had become very upset about going to school and we were quite concerned. He was performing far below his potential and his grades were not good. We knew Jeremiah was a very bright boy and that he loved learning, but school was not a place he felt safe showing that love of learning to his teachers. The different way he approached anything was usually considered a negative, nonconformist action — and conforming to expectations was the name of the game in school.

Socialization was not an especially positive experience either. Jeremiah often played alone on the playground, and the kids often teased him. Problems on the playground sometimes caused physical injuries for Jeremiah. The third grade teacher, who was Jeremiah's homeroom teacher, remarked in one of the parent-team conferences that Jeremiah was "not kind" to others because he didn't know to interact with the other children. He would play alone on the playground, instead of joining other children in organized games, for example, she said.

Consideration for gifted placement still did not come from any of these meetings. Jeremiah and we as his parents needed to be released a bit for Jeremiah's well being. It was quite difficult to get any awareness from the staff and teachers at school that many of the qualities and characteristics Jeremiah was exhibiting were typical of a highly gifted child. The pressure to conform was creating additional discomfort in what was already an almost intolerable situation.

One bright spot was that the family counselor was liked and accepted by the staff at school. Some of his suggestions were used to help Jeremiah attempt success. Unfortunately, the counselor moved out of state and was not able to continue the intervention he had begun on our son's behalf.

One policy that resulted from this intervention was that Jeremiah was given modified assignments in class and extra reading time upon completion of his class work. He could complete unfinished class work at home, and we were given a copy of the "Assertive Discipline Plan" used in class.

In April 1989, near the end of Jeremiah's third grade year, the district team (social worker, school psychologist, principal, three teachers, and the county special education association director) called a parent-team conference. We asked our attorney to be present, also, to represent Jeremiah during this meeting. Much to our surprise, Jeremiah's teachers presented us with a previously prepared letter concerning our son. They expressed concern for his welfare, both academically and behaviorally. They pointed out that they had spent hours developing and implementing plans trying to redirect his behavior, with no progress.

The teachers then recommended that Jeremiah obtain further counseling to help break the cycle of lack of progress. They also requested permission to do testing for special education. Prior to the date on the letter, Jeremiah had taken the Otis-Lennon IQ test and Iowa Test of Basic Skills. He performed well on both, excelling in science by scoring in the 99 percentile on the Iowa and again on this testing in several other areas in the 80 and 90 percentile. (Doing so near the end of his first grade year, which was a tremendously stress filled time for him.) Something had to change!

We again tried to marshal information to help Jeremiah and the school. We told school personnel we had consulted a neuro-behavioral-developmental pediatrician who planned to test Jeremiah. The district was asked to hold off on its request for testing until the results of this evaluation were available. We felt that the testing undertaken by the school would be similar to that completed at the end of first grade and the results of all that testing had been ignored, it seemed to us.

Unfortunately, the teachers didn't try to communicate with us in any way after that meeting except to send unfinished assignments home to complete. Jeremiah did unbelievable amounts of work in a short time. We knew that if all this work could be completed without problems at home, then there was not an academic problem with doing third grade work. But we did not know whether the teachers were accepting this work done at home and if so, what kind of grades he was receiving on it.

On June 5, Jeremiah went to school to pick up his report card. When he got there, he was told that he could not receive it, but his mother must go to the principal's office and get it. We were shocked to find that Jeremiah had been retained and placed in the third grade again for the next year. The retention letter was dated June 1, which was four days before Jeremiah went to get his report card. The school knew we were very much against the idea of retention; we feel that's why the principal chose not to tell us beforehand.

While we knew retention was under consideration, we had assumed that by Jeremiah's showing he could do his work at the end of the year, and having mastered the academic concepts he needed to know, there surely would be no doubt that he could do third grade work and was ready for advancement. This was particularly true in science, which would finally be a subject of study. Jeremiah was a voracious reader, and loved science, but third graders could only earn an "S" in science because it was not an academic subject yet.

The deficit areas used by our district to determine retention included the following: "following instructions, ability to complete work in class and remain on task, work independently, organizational skills to finish and return homework, participate in classroom activities, and display appropriate social behaviors." The principal stated that a parent was required to sign under "agree or disagree" with the decision to retain. I signed, with much concern, under the section for disagreeing. Retention was not an appropriate action in my view, especially considering all the information available in the five separate, though unorganized, files which the school records department kept on Jeremiah.

Gifted services were never considered as a realistic, positive way of working with Jeremiah's talents in areas where he excelled. In our discussions with school staff, it didn't seem to matter how intelligent or gifted our son might be or what his test scores indicated. No one we talked with at staff level had any awareness of what being gifted entailed. Even allowing for that lack of awareness we still didn't understand how they could think retention would ever be in Jeremiah's best intrest. How was the school going to be any more successful working with Jeremiah another year in the third grade? The principal and teachers and the school professional staff were frustrated and unable to work with him already; these same people would be attempting to teach Jeremiah third grade material again. The only change in the plan for our son was that there would be a male homeroom teacher. "Maybe that would help" was their thought.

Soon after June 5, we received a notice from the Illinois State Board of Education. It stated that our district had requested from them, on behalf of Jeremiah, a "due process" hearing to obtain our permission to allow the district to test Jeremiah. We decided to retain an attorney who would address these issues on Jeremiah's behalf.

Just before our due process hearing was scheduled to take place, on the advice of our attorney, we decided to sign the request for testing by the county special education association. We did so because we felt the reason for the hearing was to get our permission to agree to the testing, even by resorting to "due process" if necessary against us. Thus the school district would seem to be acting on behalf of and in the best interest of the child. We then would be just one of those uncooperative sets of parents schools talk about.

Just before school was to begin, we asked our attorney to arrange a meeting with the district superintendent to discuss the retention issue. In preparing for this meeting and the due process hearing before that, we had found in Jeremiah's school records, which were composed of five separate files, a very important piece of paper, the identification of Jeremiah as a gifted child in more than one area of intelligence. It was the learning disabilities resource teacher that had seen what no one else had, had identified and was willing to put it down on paper — a gifted child. He was six years old at the time of this identification.

Unfortunately, at the meeting with the district officials and our attorney, this teacher's identification was still not enough for these officials. We asked the principal at this meeting how specifically the teachers would work with Jeremiah "differently" this year than they had the previous year. The school principal, at least, could not say that "identification" had not been made by one of their own teachers. She was still in that same position in the school district, also. The administrators said that neither one of them worked there when that identification was made, so we'd have to see the retired principal if we wanted to pursue this issue. There would be no special program; the testing would determine what would be done.

We had definitely reached an impasse in this meeting. Even at the administrative level there was no awareness of what characterized giftedness. The administrator's comment was "your experts say one thing, our experts say another." Also "if there's a power conflict here, Jeremiah will not win! Our staff feels that there wouldn't be any harm in keeping Jeremiah for another year in third grade." In the district's view, retention was the best of the options considered. In fact, until Jeremiah changed there would be no attempt to find ways to help him use his potential — or even to acknowledge their own teacher's identification of giftedness. The district administrator remarked that he really had no choice but to go with their experts. To us, the district's staff were not experts at all. They didn't seem to have even the slightest knowledge about gifted children and the variety of the characteristics they exhibit. We had enlisted the services of many professionals to help our son, and also had much knowledge ourselves about what constitutes giftedness. The final comment from the school administrator was that retention was the answer their staff had come up with and "school will begin August 28."

With this impasse and no foreseeable change in awareness or attitude on anyone's part, we felt we had no choice but to teach Jeremiah at home. We knew we could not keep our son in public school because too many negative experiences associated with learning had occurred there. Our son was not happy. In order to provide a proper education, which allowed him to develop his full potential and made use of his many talents, we had to assume the responsibility of teaching Jeremiah ourselves. He is now being challenged in his academic work and is able to explore and create in a success-oriented environment. He is being instructed in English, social studies, math, language arts, science, and pursues a gifted and talented enrichment curriculum. In addition to in-home schooling, Jeremiah is being tutored at a nationally franchised educational center. Through this program, Jeremiah's strengths and weaknesses have been diagnosed, and he is progressing at his own rate of learning at his instructional level.

Fortunately for us, in Illinois, it is not difficult to establish a home school. The school system which we left at the time had no superintendent, the teachers were involved in important, unresolved contract negotiations, and the county special education association who would have been doing the testing our district requested through "due process" had not resolvevd contract issues at that time either. Our district public school system was unable to enhance educational opportunities for a child who needed more and different services. It seemed inconceivable that there could be any redeeming features causing us to trust a public school system with our child, when placing him under their leadership had enabled and even encouraged his "underachievement."

All in all, we were never successful in developing a satisfactory relationship with the school district. Because of the experiences in trying to obtain an appropriate placement for our child in a gifted program, I became an advocate for Jeremiah and an advocate for gifted and talented children. I believe that children of today definitely need advocates. Jeremiah's story is just one example of how children's rights are ignored!

Having a gifted child, one who needs more to become who he can and wants to be, means as a parent or teacher you must advocate for appropriate services for that child. There is nothing so wonderous to me as the excitement of learning through the eyes of a child who loves to explore and is gifted. The experience of being the parent of such a child has been a most precious gift to me.

The Kester Family

The Kester family lives on a farm in rural Pennsylvania, north of Pittsburgh, and approximately twenty miles east of Youngstown, Ohio. They raise beef cattle, and plant and harvest their own feed. Their son, Ted, thirteen years old, a busy seventh grader, is looking forward to summer because that includes Boy Scout camping and, above all, no school. Kelly is ten and about to complete fifth grade. She began the gifted program at the end of the fourth grade and enjoys the challenge, as well as companionship, with fellow students in the PEP program.

Cor has a master's degree in sociology, applied planning, and is currently working as the Administrator of Social and Work Related Programs for the Human Services Department. Joyce is a RN, BSN and holds a supervisory position at a large area hospital, and has recently completed her master's studies in health education.

Sixteen Heads Are Better Than One:
Collective Due Process and
A Cooperative School Administration

In October of 1988 we received a request from our daughter Kelly's fourth grade teacher for permission to have her tested for possible inclusion in the Special Education–Gifted Program. As her parents, we were proud and thrilled about this possibility and thought that we were blessed with a bright youngster. Kelly was thrilled even more, since one of her best friends was already participating in the program.

There was such a backlog of children to be tested by the psychologist that Kelly was not actually tested until January of 1989. The special education supervisor called in early February to transmit the good news that Kelly was indeed qualified for admission to the program for the gifted and to extend congratulations. We also received, at that point, the disappointing news that there would be problems for the remainder of the school year and that these would be discussed in detail at a forthcoming meeting. A follow-up letter from the supervisor informed us of a meeting to be held later that month, during which an Individual Education Program for Kelly would be discussed and planned.

Although the meeting of February 27, 1989 provided us with confirmation of Kelly's eligibility for admission to the program for the gifted, the supervisor of that program and the teacher of the gifted informed us that there would be no openings available during the remainder of the 1988–89 school year. We were also told that they could not assure us that there would be an opening available for Kelly in 1989–90. The main reason given was that the teacher of the gifted was only employed half time. To admit Kelly and the other seven students who had already qualified would mean an increase to at least three-quarter time employment, and if a majority of the six additional children scheduled for testing were to qualify for admission, the services of a full-time teacher of the gifted would be required.

They also told us that an amendment to expand the gifted education program in the school district, which had been submitted and was then pending before the Pennsylvania State Department of Education, had little chance of approval. Failure to obtain approval would mean that Kelly, the seven other children who had met admission requirements, and others who might do so, would have to remain in their regular classes at least through the 1989–90 school year without benefit of the "pullout" program for the gifted. The primary emphasis at the state level seemed to be on mainstreaming, with little attention devoted to the special and unique needs of the gifted learners.

Not wanting to place our daughter in an awkward position by asking the school district to make a single exception for her, we asked what we as parents could do to make it possible for Kelly and all other qualified children in the district to enjoy the full advantages of special provisions for the gifted. This question attracted very helpful responses, such as advising us of our rights. The supervisor of special education informed us that we could reject the proposed solution which involved an Individual Education Program to be carried out in the regular classroom and seek recourse through due process hearings. When we decided in favor of due process as a means of pressing for equal and appropriate educational opportunities for the gifted, the supervisor of special education sent us materials outlining the steps involved in this process. She also provided us with names and addresses of interested members of the legislature and of State Department of Education officials to whom we could present the case for special education in general from the point of view of parents.

My wife and I tried our best to make it very clear from the outset that all of us — parents, teachers, and administrators — were pursuing a common interest: quality education for our children and ready access by all of them to appropriate educational opportunities for which they qualify and are therefore entitled. Clearly it was established that all of us concerned were on the same side of the issue. The school district was willing to provide the special programs but could not do so without state approval and the required financial support.

In March of 1989, the State Department of Education informed our school district that approval of the amendment had been denied and instructed the district to incorporate the special provisions which had been made for the gifted into the regular classroom program. The local supervisor and our superintendent, who were supportive of our rejection of this option and understood that we planned to file for a due process hearing, immediately granted us what may be considered a pre-due process hearing. Similar prehearings were held with the parents of the seven other children who were confronted with the same dilemma.

We were invited by the superintendent of schools to the April 1989 meeting held regularly for all parents of children enrolled in the program for the gifted. A major item on the agenda called for a report on the changes taking place and a discussion of the problems anticipated in accommodating all of the children eligible for admission to the gifted program. Specific reference was made to the lack of support at the state level for specialized education for the gifted. Our attention was directed to new regulations being proposed which would greatly increase the emphasis on mainstreaming, making special education far less accessible and ignoring special needs.

Subsequent to this meeting we had several informal meetings with the superintendent and the special education supervisor. On one of these occasions, we were asked if we had any objections to having our request for a due process hearing combined with similar requests being put forward by other parents. Upon offering support for the idea of a combined effort, I was asked to serve as spokesperson for the group during the hearing. I agreed to do this if the members of the group approved.

With the eight statements of grievance treated as a single one, we received notification on April 21 that our due process hearing was scheduled for May 3. Prior to the actual hearing on that date, I met informally with the hearing officer who told me that our school district had agreed to increase the teacher's position from half to three-quarter time and admit immediately the eight qualified children to the special program for the gifted if transportation could be arranged. A response to this good news was delayed until the parents of all eight children had completed an impromptu meeting with our superintendent and the special education supervisor and had time to react to the proposed solution as a group. While the issue of the six children scheduled for testing was raised, it was getting so late in the school year that we decided to accept the terms proposed for the eight who had met all requirements and pursue with confidence the question of providing for children who meet admission requirement in the future. The due process hearing was held as scheduled but, with an agreement satisfactory to all on hand, the session was little more than a formality.

Without the cooperative and collaborative efforts of all parties in this case — teacher and supervisor, superintendent and other administrators, school board members and parents — I doubt whether these positive results could have been brought about as quickly and amiably as they were. The school board approved an increase in the teaching position independent of the State Department of Education. That action reflects the commitment to quality education and opportunities for all within our district. Despite the state's rejection of the proposed amendment to the plan for gifted education, our district continued to fund this position during the 1989–90 school year. For one overriding reason, there was no need for expensive legal services, the loss of friends and acquisition of enemies, and the ensuing long delays. From the very beginning to the conclusion, everyone involved wanted the best for our children.

The superintendent and the supervisor of special education were very helpful during this whole process. In particular, the supervisor kept all parents fully informed all along the way about developments, appeal procedures and available options. The parents worked together, rather loosely but always as a unified group when it counted.

We are confident that we would go through all of this again if a similar situation arises. We can only recommend that other parents become involved with education in general, specifically if your child is gifted or has a special need. The law in our state is on our side, and you may find that your school district personnel are too.

Anonymous

This student's father is an auctioneer and holds a college degree in economics. His mother is an active registered nurse. This student has two older brothers. For a variety of reasons, this family wishes to remain anonymous.

Challenging the Score

I received a letter from my son's school stating that, because of one test result, my son was "not an exceptional student" and thus, would not be admitted to the local gifted program called "Search." Knowing that my son had been doing extra work in school for two years, that every one of his teachers had recommended him for the program, and that test scores are not always accurate, I asked the principal if my son could monitor the program. The principal refused, while the psychologist became upset that I questioned the test result. The principal said monitoring "would make more work for me" while the psychologist stated that my son's presence would "dilute the magic" found in the group of gifted kids.

My son's school is one of the largest elementary schools in the state. Neither the principal nor the psychologist knew my son nor could recognize him on sight.

Since the priorities and points of view expressed by the principal and psychologist seemed to be way off base, I started through the recommended channels of appeal. After many meetings with the principal, psychologist, and teachers, it became apparent that despite substantial credible evidence, the administration was not going to give my son the exposure to the gifted program that I felt he deserved. I learned that, as the principal said, the decision is made "by the numbers."

It was clear from the start that the psychologist and principal were not used to anyone challenging their authority and were not open minded enough to accept any deviation from their established way of operating. The principal took credit for extra classroom work supplied by the teachers on their own. The psychologist was visibly upset when I questioned the reliability of a single IQ test and her total reliance upon that test.

After being told that the administration was "doing all the law required," I asked, "Which laws?" Upon reading the law, it was obvious the principal and psychologist did not know what they were talking about legally. The law was on my side, as were good education and common sense.

After five months of meetings with the principal, psychologist, and teachers, I requested a hearing and represented my son without assistance. I had prepared by taking comprehensive notes of all my meetings with school personnel and by obtaining copies of all my son's school records. After I'd read the law, I was able to ask pertinent questions which made me a bit more confident and gave my uneasy, upset feelings some relief. By this time, the hearing was scheduled.

During the pre-hearing conference, I read the following statement to the principal and school psychologist.

> I feel that this administration is not providing the most adequate and appropriate program to this student because mistakes have been made in the interpretation of his test score, improper evaluation of his intelligence, and failure to administer his proper placement, and all of this as a result of a deliberate, exclusionary, blind-eye policy.
>
> Working with inadequate data has led, in this case, to an improper program placement of this student. I will show by a preponderance of evidence that this school administration is neglecting its "primary responsibility for providing an appropriate program" for this student.
>
> First of all, the school psychologist made a mistake in this student's expected IQ range. Contrary to her once firm belief, this student's expected upper range IQ limit according to WISC — R is 132 and not 129. The school psychologist also implied that this student does not have a "special way of communicating" which she called "magic" that students have who scored above 130. I have three expert witnesses to testify that my son does indeed have that magic.
>
> The first witness has a broad range of experience in teaching and working with children, knows this student and recognizes firsthand this "magic" to which the school

psychologist refers because he has a tested and recorded IQ of 136. He recognizes this student as unusually special and "magic."

The other two experts are this student's current and past teachers from whom I will quote extensively later.

The teacher of the gifted and I agree that "all tests are not conclusive." The third grade teacher states that "a better criterion is needed" and that "the test is not enough" for placement of students of superior intellect such as this student.

In any borderline situation, a personal evaluation and knowledge of the student is considered essential. The fact is that placement of this student was made with no personal knowledge of this student. Only one of the people involved in this decision at the time could pick this student out of a lineup of two except by chance. And, by chance, they would be right part of the time. Just as they will be wrong part of the time by relying solely on the test numbers. The principal (3/14/89) has "used the practice of using numbers alone."

The school district points out this test fallibility in a test disclaimer that states "Remember — the above analysis may at times be contradictory, and not applicable to a given individual case. Clinical judgment must be exercised to determine relevance." The test administration further states that this test is not reliable 5 percent of the time. We have already seen mistakes made in the interpretation of the test score by the school psychologist.

This administration gives the benefit of the doubt to itself but not to the individual student and thus, in this case, is neglecting its "primary responsibility for providing an appropriate program" for this student.

Mistakes made by other administration officials are the result of unfamiliarity with proper placement procedures and lack of knowledge of actual classroom situations. The principal gave me incorrect information as to what would constitute an adequate prehearing conference and had to correct himself later.

He also offered to this student as "extra educational opportunities for him within the classroom," opportunities, most of which he has been utilizing for almost two years. The only "extras" are some previously unavailable pamphlets, games, and problems which are to be self-administered. Self instruction by this third grader is not adequate extra opportunity. Computer instruction has not been implemented as "the games are missing" according to the student.

In direct contradiction to the principal's statement of 3/14/89 to "start them today," no extra opportunities for this student have been made available.

Apparently, the principal does not know that this student's teacher "doesn't have enough time to devote to" my son (a note of 3/20/89) in his classroom and states that this student usually chooses appropriate reading material to fill extra time. The principal's offer of "extra educational opportunities" turns out to be vacuous, inadequate, inappropriate self-instruction, and for the most part, not even extra. This demonstrates a lack of knowledge by him of what has been happening in this student's classroom for almost two years.

These inappropriate situations and proven mistakes are amplified by this administration's 100 percent reliance on a test score that is not 100 percent reliable and then using that test score solely and completely as an exclusionary device. Total reliance on a score that is self-admittedly not 100 percent reliable will *undeniably* lead to mistakes. This deliberate blind-eye exclusionary practice is unbecoming an academic institution and is a totally inappropriate basis for individual academic decisions.

Administrative ease is served nicely by this policy. After all, to look beyond a fallible test score would, according to the principal (1/26/89) "make more work for me." But administrative ease should not take precedence over individual educational decisions. This student has a *right* to an individual academic decision, not an administrative policy decision.

The inappropriate administrative policy of blind-eye exclusion has resulted in an inadequate placement of this student. Justice should be blind, education should not be blind. This test was intended by all to be a guide, not a basis for automatic exclusion.

Following is a succinct list of reasons why the Search program is the most appropriate and adequate program for this student:

1. My son has tested in the "superior range" (quotes from test results).

2. IQ range overlaps state mandated inclusion score. It is possible this student could have an IQ ten points higher than one who scored 130.

3. He has earned straight A's since first grade.

4. He has demonstrated his ability to handle, with ease and enthusiasm, more extracurricular activities than most students.

5. Parents have evidence of student being "overtly eager" for more academic industry with high self-motivation sufficient for more academic instruction, not self-instruction.

6. Current administration exclusion policy differs from previous administrations at the same school, differs from some other schools, and is different than the state mandate. The state sets a minimum number of students for inclusion while the school uses that as a maximum. One wonders what the stance of this administration would be if the state did not mandate a minimum for inclusion.

7. My son's "magic" is such that he would fit in and benefit and, the group would benefit too. I have quotes to support this assumption.

8. Psychologist stated that any extra programs for my son should be "rigorous" (1/26/89). The Search program is most "rigorous" and certainly more adequate than the current program.

9. He has a Slosson IQ of 137;

10. Teacher's comments after test results were known, such as:

   a. Richard is a special case who would benefit from and has the ability to handle the Search program with no problem. Search is a program more adequate and appropriate than the one he is currently receiving.

   b. He definitely could handle the work in Search. He has special communication and understanding abilities which are not being fully utilized because his regular classroom teacher doesn't have enough time to devote to him in class.

   c. All tests are not conclusive. Other quotes are available and will be used if necessary.

11. My son, for reasons other than the state mandate of a 130 IQ admittance score, should be placed in the Search program because of what is being offered by the school.

The Search program is the most appropriate and adequate for this student. This program may be mandated by the state for other students and other students may be called "gifted," but by the preponderance of evidence here presented — evidence negative, positive, personal, educational, and esoteric — it is clear and emphatic that the Search program is the most appropriate and adquate program for this student.

This administration has reached a general policy decision, now it is time for this administration to reach a specific educational and academic decision on an individual student. I call on this administration to fulfill their "primary responsibility for providing an appropriate program" for this student — in the form of the Search program.

At the closed hearing, which was at my request, I was on one side of the room with one witness, because the principal would allow only one teacher at a time and I had called two teachers as witnesses. The administration trooped in with five: the principal, the psychologist, the vice principal, the teacher of the gifted, and their "outside expert" from the intermediate unit to do the questioning.

Before I was done cross-examining the first witness, she reversed herself several times and the hearing officer expressed surprise at the administration procedure.

After I got on the record that no one knew my son, that the exclusionary decision was based on a single test, that three teachers' recommendations were ignored, that the multidisciplinary team that made the decision did not include the student's teacher, and that neither parental input nor achievement tests were considered, the hearing officer recessed the hearing to call for "sufficient and current information" to be obtained to help him make a decision on my son's giftedness. I objected that this was exactly what I was there to provide if I could only call my own witnesses. Nevertheless, he called for more testing. As I could not legally refuse without jeopardizing my goals, I agreed, with the stipulation that the testing was to be done out of the area so that the current psychologist or administration could not influence the outcome in any way.

Thus, the hearing officer arranged for me to travel one and one half hours to Pennsylvania State University for extensive testing of my son's intelligence.

All tests given over a full day came back above the state guidelines for the gifted classification (IQ 130). Two IQ tests and several achievement tests proved that my feelings of what was right for my son were correct. The same test he had taken earlier came back 13 points higher — thus proving that IQ test results will vary as conditions and time vary.

The administration withdrew and the following school year placed my son in the gifted program. The principal and psychologist have given my case to a new vice principal and have not contacted me since then. I'm still not sure that they know what they were doing wrong in this case as the hearing officer was not explicit in rendering his decision.

I would somehow like to make sure that the principal now knows that judging the intelligence of a student solely on the basis of one test or on one type of test is unfair, not legal in this state, against the interests of good education, and against the interests of the student. However, being realistic, I fear retaliation against my son and his brothers by the administration. Any closed mind is diminished, and small minds will retaliate. The minds of the principal and psychologist were not open minds.

The teachers in this case were mostly understanding and sympathetic and welcomed my challenge of the administration. I await visible changes at my son's school.

The advice to other parents would be to know your rights, not to be intimidated by the administration, listen to and get advice from several teachers who know the student. Be prepared to have the administration assume an adversarial position against the student and expect all the administration to hang together. Know the law and know the student.

The Fink Family

John and Suzanne Fink live in Wharton, Texas. John received his medical degree from the University of Michigan and Suzanne holds a nursing diploma from York Hospital School of Nursing. Dr. Fink spends his free time running marathons and participating in church activities. Suzanne is a hospital volunteer and also serves as a substitute teacher in the local school district's special education program for the handicapped. In addition to Ashley, the family has a second child, Blair, who is seven.

Ashley is enjoying her gifted education instruction and when not excelling in intellectual pursuits, keeps busy by participating in all types of community sports activities.

The $23,000 Square Root
of the Standard Deviation

In July 1989 we received a brief note indicating that our daughter Ashley had been nominated, but did not meet the criteria, for the gifted/talented program which begins in the third grade. She had made straight A's through first and second grade, and we had been told repeatedly by all of her teachers that she was one of the best students. My wife, Suzanne, called the principal who pointed out that she had nothing to do with the process of selecting students for the gifted program. The superintendent had sole responsibility. Suzanne called the superintendent and was told, "I don't see anything you can do to change the situation."

We made an appointment and met with the principal and superintendent. They indicated that there was a matrix, which took into account several criteria, and that Ashley didn't make "the cut." We were told she "could" be considered next year. We had Ashley evaluated by a psychologist who was approved by the school district. After administering an intelligence test, he reported that her full scale IQ was 139. The psychologist agreed that Ashley belonged in any and all enrichment programs for the gifted. She was bright, got straight A's, was never a behavior problem, was active in swimming and soccer teams, and participated in school and community fund raising activities. Still Ashley didn't meet the "cutoff" on the matrix.

Ashley was crushed when she learned that she was not to be in the gifted program. She wanted to know why, and we couldn't explain it to her satisfaction, because we didn't understand ourselves. During the school year, most of her friends were in the program. Ashley frequently came home crying because she couldn't get computer time as did her friends, or couldn't do a project or go on a special trip with the gifted students, etc. It was hard for us to understand why an obviously bright child should be denied further enrichment because she didn't make an artificial "cut."

The superintendent stated she had not done well enough on the four parts of the achievement test, which constituted four of the seven items included in the "matrix." The other three components were two teacher recommendations and a score on an intelligence test.

The students individual scores on the "matrix" were added together and a mean score was obtained. We were told that a standard deviation was calculated, added to the mean, and this was the cutoff point that determined which of the students were excluded. John requested and received the list of scores of the nomination group for 1989, and later for the 1988 and 1987 groups. He did the computations and statistics, and the results were not the same as the superintendent's for any one of these three groups of students. He took the results to the head of the math department at the local junior college. He concurred with John's computations. There was a large discrepancy in the number of students accepted during the three years. If Ashley's score had been considered during any one of the previous three years, she would have been admitted in the gifted program.

We asked to be on the school board agenda and after presenting a lengthy appeal, we were thanked for our presentation. There were no questions asked, nor discussion, and the board members immediately went to the next item of business. We sought legal counsel, appealed to the board again on the discrepancy between the superintendent's number and the correct number. We were then told that the square root of one standard deviation was added to the mean and the discussion was closed. It didn't matter that no one on the school board had ever heard of "square root of the standard deviation." Another door was closed.

It was apparent that the superintendent and school board had had enough of us and weren't interested in discussing this matter any further. They did not inform us that we had any avenue of appeal or that due process was available. Later, we learned that we had such protection and that we could appeal to the State Board of Education. Out of frustration, we filed a civil suit for our child and other children denied additional enrichment in the gifted program in our system.

In our complaint we stated that the selection process was flawed, unfair, and it inappropriately excluded our daughter. We felt our legal action would be viewed very negatively by our friends who are teachers and school administrators, our other professional friends, fellow church members, etc. Quite the opposite. Many people contacted us with wishes of support and encouragement to push onward. Strangers stopped us to say they were behind us and even an elderly woman at a funeral whispered to me that we were right and we should not stop. We did not receive a single negative comment from anyone. We contacted the two most notable expert witnesses in gifted education in the state of Texas and gave them copies of everything. They were very eager to help us. They both felt strongly that the selection process was flawed and that it inappropriately excluded our daughter. The school board indicated at the pretrial meeting that Ashley would not be designated as gifted but that she could attend the gifted classes and activities if we dropped the suit. They would not consider the three students whose matrix scores were equal to or above Ashley's, but below the cutoff. We would not consider their offer.

We applied for a pretrial hearing to get an injunction to place Ashley in the gifted program so she wouldn't miss any more time in the program while we awaited trial. The day of the trial came and the expert witnesses were impeccable, impressible, or impressive and unshakable. The superintendent admitted there was not another child in the third grade with a higher IQ than Ashley, and he stumbled over contradictory statements. He admitted that Ashley showed superior aptitude in mathematics and that the state directions designated that students who show a "superior aptitude in any aspect" should be included in a gifted program. The school board's "expert witness" from Region III was confused, lost her composure, and provided little or no support for the school district position. The president of the school board admitted he was not familiar with the gifted selection process and did not review it prior to the hearing. The court recorder indicated to our attorney that the district judge had made up his mind and continued testimony was unnecessary. We rested our case. The judge said he felt Ashley should be in the program, that "she had fallen through the cracks," that we would most probably win the case, but "he was not going to play God and place her in the program." He instructed both sets of attorneys to settle this soon and he would arrange for a speedy trial within thirty days. We felt devastated that the judge had no backbone when he had admitted he felt Ashley should be in the program.

After a three-way phone conversation among our local lawyer, the Houston Law firm of the school board, and the judge the next day, we were notified that they were petitioning for the case to be moved to federal court in Corpus Christi because some of the wording in our complaint indicated that civil rights could be a consideration. This would involve a minimum of seven months to get the trial underway and by that time the school year would be over. Furthermore, a tremendous cost would have been involved. Everyone felt this was a ploy by the school board's attorneys to get out of a losing battle in the district court.

Many people were appalled at the treatment we received. We had spent over $23,000 to date, and we were exhausted.

We had kept the whole process secret from Ashley. We almost moved over the school situation.

While our case was pending, the State of Texas promulgated new guidelines for gifted education programs. In response to these new guidelines, a committee was formed to create standards for selection in our local district's gifted education program. We were selected to participate and the committee constructed a new set of selection criteria. After the new standards were in place, we filed a motion for the dismissal of the case.

Ashley easily met the criteria of the gifted selection process at the fourth grade level and is doing extremely well. The superintendent resigned and is in charge of the new teacher orientation in another school district.

Our new selection process for the gifted program is broad based. It includes consideration of the past grade point average, has alternate tests if a consideration of racial/ethnic bias is present, and includes a parent checklist/nomination form.

Would we do it again? Yes! Most people would not have the financial means or would possibly be swayed by thoughts of negative reactions from family, friends, community, etc. If we cannot make the world a better place for our children, we are not doing all we can for them.

Part II

Receiving Appropriate
Instruction

The Lindblad Family

John Lindblad received his M.D. from the University of Pittsburgh School of Medicine. He and Jeanette were married in 1964 after he completed his pediatric residency at Children's Hospital of Pittsburgh. The Lindblads spent two years in Montgomery, Alabama, courtesy of the United States Air Force. John began his private practice in 1966 and works 80–90 hours a week. He is also an avid gardener and a United States Swimming referee. He has managed to attend most of the meets all three children entered over the past fifteen years.

Jeanette has a bachelor of science degree from Carnegie Mellon University. When she's not driving "Mom's Taxi," she does the office bookkeeping or any of the other tasks necessary to enable all these overachievers to overachieve. Before they were married, Jeanette worked for the Richard King Mellon Foundation in Pittsburgh. Both Dr. and Mrs. Lindblad excelled in math.

Douglas, twenty-five, completed his first year at Baylor College of Medicine. He now attends Rice University where he will get his master's in electrical engineering, followed by his Ph.D. He will then return to Baylor to finish medical school. He has temporarily retired from competitive swimming and no longer has time for his clarinet or piano.

Lauren, seventeen, is completing her senior year in high school. She is in three Advanced Placement courses, plays violin in the high school orchestra, and spends four hours a day six days a week swimming on a highly competitive swim team at the University of Pittsburgh.

Eric, twenty-one, is attending Princeton and has been accepted into the Woodrow Wilson School of Public and International Affairs. He continues to study economics and will add government and politics.

The Road from Mediocrity to Princeton

I think I should state several facts before discussing our due process hearings. First, we have three gifted children: Douglas, born in 1966; Eric, born in 1970; and Lauren, born in 1973. Of the three, only Lauren's needs have been met in any way by the school district, though her needs in mathematics were, and are, as neglected as the math needs of any other gifted child in this district. Douglas was extremely frustrated by the lack of challenge, and frankly, it was Eric who saved Doug. I say that because Doug participated in the tutoring we arranged privately for Eric and Doug probably benefitted more from it than did Eric. Douglas learned how to work independently, and how to teach himself.

Second, when I speak of our frustration with Eric's education, I realize that his case is very unusual because he is "severely gifted." Parents reading his case history should not compare their child to Eric and feel they cannot ask for the kind of environment suitable for their gifted child. Other highly gifted students might achieve as much or even more and still others less, but no child does well without sufficiently high goals and the opportunity to learn. Limits should not be set on excellence and achievement.

Over the years, many people have said we should not expect the public schools to educate a child like Eric. Eric is a normal boy with the same interests as other boys. He loves sports, whether it's football, hockey, or tennis. He swam competitively for eleven years, received four varsity letter awards in high school — he even qualified for the regional meet in the 100 yard butterfly. He took piano lessons for nine years. Eric excelled in all subject areas, but had one terrible sin: being a genius in mathematics. He did his best to keep this talent hidden from his chronological peers; and he is basically a very private person.

The hearings occurred because the district denied what Eric was, failed to give us the facts, covered up evidence of his ability, tried extremely hard to make him average, used him over and over to bring home glory for the district, but eventually punished him for daring to excel. His story is a good example of the worst an educational system can do to its best students.

Third, this district has a large number of gifted students, approximately 10 percent of each grade level. When Eric was in elementary school, the average IQ at that school was 116; this is very high. It was obvious that many other students were not being challenged. Most parents did not ask for a due process hearing because they feared reprisals and justly so. Some parents could not afford an attorney, taught their children outside the classroom, were apathetic, sent them to private schools, or had them skip grades and/or graduate early. In one case, every weekend for two years, the parents drove their mathematically precocious son from Pittsburgh to Baltimore so that he might participate in Johns Hopkins accelerated Saturday math classes.

Fourth, most of the mathematically gifted in our district attend fast-paced math classes during the summers following seventh and eight grades, either at one of the Johns Hopkins Programs or at the local Community College of Allegheny County–South Campus. These students must then choose between repeating a whole year of math that they know well (a real waste of time and talent) or they accelerate and (as with Doug, Eric, and Lauren) lose the honors math credit their less able or less motivated classmates receive. The latter decision lowers their quality point average and class rank and severely affects merit scholarship opportunities. Either decision carries a stiff penalty. The marvelous experience of learning math with other gifted students at an appropriate level and pace far outweighs a lot of disadvantages.

Learning is what is is meant to be: exciting, challenging, and satisfying.

Finally, here are some of the facts the district's administrators knew before Eric even entered kindergarten: the most glaring is that at age five his test scores clearly established that he was already achieving at a general grade level of 2.9, which means the ninth month of the second grade. His test scores were as follows:

Nursery school: Age 5.0

Stanford-Binet: 139

Wide-Range Achievement Test (WRAT):

   Reading Grade Equivalent   4.2

   Math Grade Equivalent   3.0

Gray Oral Reading: Grace Equivalent   2.9

Kindergarten: Age 6.0

WRAT: Reading Grade Equivalent   5.0

           Math Grace Equivalent   4.7

Gray Oral Reading: Grade Equivalent   5.5

Weschler Intelligence Scale for Children–Revised (WISC-R): Arithmetic Subtest Mental age = 11.6

          (Math IQ = 192)

Stanford Achievement Test:

   Primary Level II:

     Math Concepts   Grade Equivalent   4.2

   Primary Level III:

     Math Concepts   Grade Equivalent   3.5

     Math Applications   Grade Equivalent   3.7

   Intermediate I:

     Math Computation Grade Equivalent   6.1

Slosson Intelligence Test: IQ = 159

Key Math Diagnostic Arithmetic Test:

   Grade Equivalent   4.1

The last two tests were administered by the district. You can see that it should have been abundantly clear to any

"educator" that this child had unusual ability. The progress
Eric made in one year without any formal education is amazing. He should have been valued and encouraged to achieve.
Instead, the first three years were devoted to slowing Eric's
progress, to denying he had any unusual ability, but most of
all, to avoiding any responsibility for meeting his academic
needs.

Perhaps I should give a little background about this particular school. It was newly constructed when Doug entered
kindergarten; it was designed for open classrooms with
neither walls nor doors. We were told that Doug would be
placed with other students functioning at the same ability
level as he. Unfortunately, this never happened. The faculty
and administration were operating in the same rigid fashion
seen elsewhere; those teachers who dared to allow children
to learn at their own rate were severely criticized and the
children penalized. Eventually, permanent "temporary"
walls were installed and the building became as rigid as the
curriculum. Ironically, the artificial walls interfered with
the architect's heating and cooling system in the same way
the inflexible curriculum created walls that squelched learning for the gifted. Math, of course, wasn't the only area
deprived, but it is somewhat easier to learn independently
in other areas.

Since Douglas was our first child, we were new at the
game and naive. We kept believing the educational hogwash
because we felt that professionals would have the best interests of children at heart. We didn't know that children have
little to do with the politics and power struggles among
administration, staff, and school board.

We soon learned that we weren't taken seriously when
we presented evidence of Eric's needs or of Doug's. Educators
have a habit of speaking to parents as if they are the same
age as their children. While we did not enjoy being adver-

saries, we had children who wanted and loved to learn, who were being systematically stifled, and who had no one else to champion them. If I told the principal that Doug was so bored with second, third, or fourth grade math that he refused to prove once again that he could multiply, I was viewed as an obnoxious parent pampering her child. When I told him that Eric, in kindergarten, was doing Doug's fourth grade homework assignment every night, I am sure he did not believe me. Doug's teacher knew the primitive printing was not Doug's writing and wasn't very happy about it.

While we were on the verge of a due process hearing several times with Doug, Eric's giftedness was so extreme that we finally had his first hearing, which ran from May through July 1979. The principal had insisted upon Eric's taking the Differential Aptitude Test in June following second grade. He administered it himself over a three-day period and said it would tell us what should be planned for third grade. The DAT is a test normally given at the end of eighth grade and measures mechanical ability, numerical ability, and abstract reasoning ability. The district hoped to prove, we learned later, that Eric was carefully tutored in math and not truly gifted.

A representative from Johns Hopkins University promised the district that they would interpret his scores and if, as the district believed, his ability was the result of home tutoring, he would score high in numerical and mechanical and low in abstract. His scores were kept secret for the next seven and a half months. We could not understand this until, on January 23, 1979, we finally saw the scores. Eric had scored in the 25th percentile in mechanical reasoning, 45th percentile in numerical reasoning, and 99 + percentile, which is the ceiling of the test, in abstract reasoning. All these scores were according to eighth grade norms — six years ahead of his age group. At this point, we filed for a hearing.

We hired an attorney who represented the teacher's union. He said he could represent us because we were arguing program and not picking on a teacher. He felt we had a very strong case and prepared for the hearing. Following disclosure, during which each side sees the other's evidence, the district persuaded the teacher's union to remove our attorney from the case. He was notified on the day of the hearing that this was a conflict of interest. He had no choice but to withdraw, since we could not compete with the huge retainer he received from the union. We had one week to find a new attorney and the one we found was totally incompetent, which, of course, was exactly what the district hoped.

During the hearing, teacher after teacher spent hours in what was obviously carefully rehearsed testimony with visual aids of many kinds, reiterating the district's position that fifth grade math was appropriate for Eric and the rest of his program in reading, spelling, etc. was even more appropriate. The principal testified, under oath, that he did not recall giving Eric the DAT in June nor could he remember when the scores were received. The date was stamped on the test. The district never asked the representative from Johns Hopkins University to interpret the scores. We contacted Johns Hopkins and were advised that Eric was ready for secondary math, specifically Algebra I, an acceleration of five years. This information was not accepted as evidence, however, because we had no expert witness from the university there to testify and the district could not cross-examine. The school psychologist said the DAT should be disregarded because there were no norms for seven year olds. Of course, how could there be? Very few students this age have ever had reason to take this test.

The representative from Johns Hopkins had also recommended that Eric be given the STEP (Sequential Test of Educational Progress) and gave the district's psychologist specific instructions about how it was to be administered and scored. He ignored those instructions, yet Eric still scored in the 98th and 99th percentile at the twelfth grade level in computation and concepts. During the hearing, the fifth grade math teacher pointed out that the STEP test didn't ask Eric to identify numbers in the billions; therefore, Eric didn't know how to do that. Since fifth grade math teaches that, fifth grade is appropriate. The same logic was applied to other minor items the test did not include. No one cared that Eric could identify numbers in the billions by age five.

When Eric was given the STEP, the psychologist also administered the Wechsler Intelligence Scale for Children. Eric came home that day and said, "I don't think he liked giving me that test." When I questioned him, he told me the psychologist kept looking at his watch, clearing his throat, tapping his pencil, getting up and walking behind Eric, and doing other things which seemed intended to distract Eric. I was hardly surprised when the IQ was reported as 127 and the district said they would present evidence in the hearing that Eric was not gifted. The district uses a 130 IQ cutoff. We took Eric to another school psychologist one month later who gave him a Stanford-Binet. Eric scored 145 IQ and the tester, who knew nothing about Eric's situation said, "Mrs. Lindblad, this boy has exceptional ability in mathematics; I've never seen a third grader respond as he does." I said, "Yes, I know." I could have cried.

We had had considerable evaluation done by a psychologist in a small rural district. He was called to his superintendent's office shortly before the hearing and ordered not to testify in Eric's behalf. Our district had made calls to the superintendent and had made specific threats. When we tried to introduce into evidence his superior test scores, the evidence was not allowed as the tester couldn't be cross-examined. At this point, let me say that a due process hearing is supposed to be an administrative hearing, not a formal trial.

During the hearing, we bcame aware that the hearing officer had a professional relationship with the school district's psychologist. He was the mentor for the psychologist's Ph.D. candidacy. I overheard them planning their regular luncheon date. The hearing officer should have disqualified himself.

The head of the mathematics department at Carnegie Mellon University had administered the math portion of the Scholastic Aptitude Test to Eric at age eight. His score was 520. The average college-bound senior scores 494. Again, this evidence was disregarded because no one from the Educational Testing Service was present to testify and there were no known norms for an eight year old.

Perhaps I should interject at this point why fifth grade math was not appropriate for Eric. The first-grade teacher had taught Eric math in kindergarten and first grade. She covered the majority of the fourth grade math program with him by the end of first grade. She told me that he was the epitome of a "truly gifted child."

In the second grade, Eric's homeroom teacher was given the task of continuing his independent learning program. At the same time, she was to teach the bottom math class. She had no more than five minutes a day to spend with him. The other students resented Eric's beating them at math games and Eric soon developed stomach pains every morning and did not want to go to school. Finally, in February, my promise that I would come to school so he could learn, convinced him to go out the door. I discovered that Eric could consume the entire week's lesson plans in twenty minutes. After two weeks, a volunteer teacher was located and she completed most of the fifth grade book with him. She was upset because both the fifth and sixth grade books had very little new material in them. Therefore, when the hearing was held in the spring of third grade, Eric had spent the year in remedial fifth grade math.

The hearing officer did not render his decision until September 11, 1979, which, of course, was now Eric's fourth grade year. It was his decision that Eric attend fifth grade math. Eric had attended fifth grade math in third grade, sitting on the floor in the back of the room working in an independent program covering the same concepts he had mastered years before. He was tested every eight cards but never told the results as the teacher didn't have an answer key. This was not education at its finest.

I would like to mention at this point that our daughter qualified for the gifted program at age five but she was refused admission to the district's program. We were told she was shy and lacked confidence, as if this has anything to do with ability. She was finally admitted in third grade; she also excels in math although not to the degree Eric does. Her 720 on the SAT-M in ninth grade indicates very high ability.

We hired a new attorney after the decision, and he filed an appeal. He also addressed the fact that Eric was tested in reading by the district in order to place him in an appropriate class. He was placed in a class four levels (more than one year's work) below the reading level determined by the placement test. The reason given was, "That is where everyone else his age is, and we don't want to make Eric different." Another problem he addressed was that Eric was required to earn 95 percent on all math pretests (in order to skip material he already knew well). To make sure this was impossible, the pretests had no more than twelve problems; one error would be 92 percent. All of the legal appeals, etc. took months.

By fourth grade, we knew we had to do something positive to combat all the negative experiences Eric was having at school. In second grade, Eric had attended a math group about once a month that consisted of his brother and some other sixth-grade students. The man teaching the group was very good with them and enjoyed gifted students. We asked him if he would tutor Eric. He began by giving Eric an achievement test for Algebra I. Eric tested out of Algebra I. The tutor agreed to begin *The Elements of Mathematics* program with both Eric and Doug. Written for gifted secondary school students, this program is based on thinking in-depth rather than acceleration through the standard textbooks. A third boy who was Doug's age was included in the class. Eric thrived! All three loved the class and worked very hard and achieved highly. Every time the tutor thought he knew just where Eric was functioning, his comprehension and insight would make another giant leap. He received his first college credits for a logic course before he was ten years old. His SAT-M at age nine was 570.

During the summer following fourth grade, Eric attended computer science and problem solving classes at Carnegie Mellon University with a group of gifted seventh grade students. He earned three credits.

Back at school, Eric had spent fourth grade in sixth grade math placement, waiting for the legal skirmishes to be resolved. The teacher would say things to him like, "I suppose you have a minus zero on your homework again, Eric. Who did it this time — you or Doug?" Eric couldn't understand why she thought Doug had time to do *his* work. She would say, "The fourth grader in here got a minus zero on the test. What is the matter with you sixth graders?" It did not endear him to the class. Eric is very quiet and never told me about these comments; other mothers called and told me their son or daughter was in the class and upset by the remarks.

September 25, 1980 was the date of the second hearing. The district wanted to transport Eric to the junior high school for Algebra II. We, and the psychologist who tested him, felt that he would be socially and emotionally uncomfortable. We requested that a secondary teacher be brought to the elementary school one hour a week to teach Eric. Since the gifted program had a math specialist at the secondary level, this would not have been difficult. We knew that Eric did not need 180 days to learn Algebra II and that the teacher had had no experience with a child his age. The added negative factor was that this was Doug's class. Doug was attending honors geometry at the high school because he had skipped fifth grade math, but the students in this class were his peers.

This hearing officer was much more familiar with gifted students and seemed to listen carefully to all the evidence. He apparently tried to make both sides of the dispute happy. He did order that Eric attend Algebra II at the junior high but he also ordered that remediation be done on the algebraic areas he had missed (it was now November) and that the district tutor Eric an additional two and a half hours per week at his elementary school. Eric spent three weeks in the Algebra II class where no remediation was done. He was very uncomfortable with the comments of the other students; he began having stomach pains again; and he was not able to write fast enough. Eric's tutor went to talk to the teacher and tried to explain that Eric had a ten-year-old's hand coordination because he was ten-years-old. He told her that Eric could factor polynomials in his head and did not need to write down all fourteen steps. She could not accept this. We finally refused permission for him to be transported.

Meanwhile, Eric was being "tutored" for two and a half hours per week. Because no one at the elementary school had secondary certification in math, it was decided that the teacher of the gifted would teach Eric computer science. She had taken six Saturday classes in a class taught by Eric's tutor, strangely enough. Eric had three credits from Carnegie Mellon University, one of the top computer science universities in the country. It still could have been a worthwhile experience except for one thing. Eric had to log in at the computer room at 12:10 P.M. every day and sit there in a room without windows, with nothing at all to do, and was not permitted to use the computer until she returned from lunch at 12:50 P.M. She then spent ten minutes on the computer. Not only was Eric missing the socialization of his classmates during lunch and recess, he sat alone wasting his time in solitary confinement. We wrote to the regional reviewer who was supposed to see that the hearing officer's decision was carried out. When she investigated, she said the log book showed that Eric received fifty minutes of instruction each day. Eric asked why she did not believe what he told her. I had no way to answer that. At our insistence, the computer "lessons" ended. Eric had no math at school the remaining five months of the year.

Something wonderful happened soon after. Eric had scored 650 on the SAT-M as a ten-year-old and during the summer following fifth grade, he participated in a fast-paced math program at the Community College of Allegheny County– South Campus. He completed Algebra II in five class days; he led this class of gifted eighth and ninth graders. He loved it! Doug spent the same five days covering Algebra III and then both boys spent three days in Trigonometry. Both did exceptionally well on the national tests given at the end of the eight weeks. Doug skipped eleventh grade math and returned to tenth grade placement with twelfth grade Advanced Placement Calculus as his math course. The next two years I drove him to the University of Pittsburgh and Carnegie Mellon where his senior year he was the first high school student invited to participate in their honors math class. School personnel lectured me on how I had warped Eric by making him go to school in the summer but I knew this was right for Eric, so I no longer cared.

During the sixth grade, the head of the math department at the high school offered to tutor Eric first period two days a week in tenth grade geometry. We drove him to the high school and back prior to the start of school for the elementary students. He finished the course with a 99 percent. He also scored 720 on the SAT-M at age eleven.

The next summer, Eric went back to CCAC and completed Algebra III in five class days. Once again he led the class and loved it! He and Doug also earned three more college credits in *The Elements of Mathematics*: Logic and Sets, and Introduction to Fields. In seventh grade, Eric took a functions course second semester at the high school with the eleventh graders. By this time Eric was closer to them in size, the students were more mature, Eric had been attending math competitions with them for a couple of years, and the teacher was more flexible. There were no problems. He also was the only one of the 16,000 gifted students participating in Johns Hopkins Talent Search to score a perfect 800 on the SAT-M. In eighth grade he took Advanced Placement Calculus and scored a 5 on the AP exam.

From second grade on, Eric won nearly every math contest in which the district entered him. He won Calcu-Solve Tournaments, Equations Tournaments, Math Wizard, and the Sixth Grade Math Contest. He was the district's highest scorer in the Algebra I contest when he was in fifth grade, placed first in the statewide math contest in both seventh and eighth grades, won local math league competitions, Pennsylvania Math League competitions, calculus competitions. From the eighth grade on he placed in the top six and up in ten high school math competitions at various universities; was on the fourth place team representing Pennsylvania at the Atlantic Region Mathematics League Competition (ARML); won awards at Shippensburg University in yearly contests sponsored by the Pennsylvania Council of

Teachers of Mathematics; was named the top math student by the Western Pennsylvania Council of Teachers of Mathematics and by the Pennsylvania Council of Teachers of Mathematics; was selected for the Pennsylvania Governor's School for the Sciences as one of the top ninety in the state, for the Research Science Institute as one of the top thirty-five students in the country; was a National Merit Finalist; was the top scorer in both junior and senior high in the American High School Math Exam; and participated well enough on the American Invitational Mathematics Exam to qualify for the USA Mathematical Olympiad Exam. He was invited and did attend the United States Mathematical Olympiad Training Program at West Point as one of the top twenty-four math students in the country.

The district's reaction to this great honor was to mark him absent for the days that he missed school. Each time he won, an article appeared in the newspaper identifying his school as winning again. When he went to many of these contests, we drove the math team and were the only team present without a school representative. I can't imagine the district sending the football team to a game without the coach.

I have listed all these awards, not to brag about Eric, but to show that he generated a lot of favorable publicity for the district. When he entered high school, there were no more math courses available and the district, as usual, abdicated any responsibility. For four years I drove him to Carnegie Mellon University where he received A's in eight college math courses; by his senior year he had a total of thirty-two credits in mathematics.

But he had no high school math credits and the state requires two in order to graduate. That requirement is now three. The high school courses taken in elementary and junior high partially fulfilled the state's requirements for those grade levels. His college courses were listed on his high school transcript but he received no credit for them. We asked that he receive credit for them because the district had, for seventeen years, granted credit for Hebrew classes taken at a nonaccredited private school, had been granting credits for courses taken by students participating in Outward Bound, and certainly a university of Carnegie Mellon's stature should be accepted too. The request was denied. We asked that the district provide appropriate math courses for Eric on his Individualized Educational Program for his senior year. They refused. We asked for a hearing.

This time we had no attorney. The hearing took place on January 21, February 4, and March 3, 1988. Since we were well into his senior year, we asked that his college courses in which he was now enrolled be on his transcript, that these and his other college courses be added into his grade point average, and that the current courses be on his IEP. Since Eric had no math credits, his grade point average and class rank were lower than his classmates who had not accelerated. It seemed unfair that Eric, who had a 97 percent overall average in all his other courses, was not first or second in his class merely because he had no math. Class rank, unfortunately, is a big factor in scholarship awards.

One of the most upsetting things to me during the hearing was that although the district told the state that Eric spent 10 percent of his in-school time involved in gifted education, he actually spent less than 1 percent. This 10 percent figure was sent to the state for reimbursement. When I asked how they could possibly justify the 9 percent they were not providing, the district's testimony was that the 9 percent was the time he spent at Carnegie Mellon. In other words, they were paid for what we provided.

During the hearing, the hearing officer ordered the district to test Eric to determine where he was mathematically. This

was done by a professor at Carnegie Mellon. The test showed
he was functioning on the level of a college senior. The
hearing officer's decision was that the district should put
the two courses from his senior year on his transcript, in
his IEP, and that they should be added into his grade point
average. The district appealed the last part and won; they
did not object to the first two parts of the order. About a
month later, it occurred to their attorney that if the courses
were on Eric's IEP, the district must pay for them. So the
district appealed. They lost and then appealed to the Com-
monwealth Court and lost again. They asked for a new hearing to argue reimbursement and were told that they knew,
or should have known, that they were responsible for anything on the IEP. We finally received $2,300 in March, 1990;
not enough to cover legal fees, but a moral victory nonethe-
less.

While this was going on, graduation day arrived. We didn't
know until one hour before the ceremony whether Eric
should even go. His diploma was not legal because he had
no math credits; the hearing officer had ordered that the two
CMU courses would fulfill the state's math requirement,
but he had not yet received credit for them. He still has not
two years later. He did go to graduation but it was very
depressing; no one felt good about being there; we had no
celebration planned. The attorney from the Department of
Education called and told Eric to go, that it was not his fault
and he should not be punished further.

Eric was named a Princeton Scholar as one of the top
seventy applicants out of 12,000. His high school library was
given $250 in his honor because of the school district's com-
mitment to academic excellence. Princeton called us about
this award and we could have asked them not to make the
award, but that would have punished the students and not
those who are responsible.

Eric is now a sophomore at Princeton University, majoring in economics. He dropped mathematics! Princeton refused to grant him any credit for the thirty-two credits he had at Carnegie Mellon. They don't accept any outside credits. In order to obtain an undergraduate mathematics degree at Princeton, he would have to take eight more math courses, most of which would be at the graduate level. Once again, Eric was to be punished for accelerating. His classmates will receive a math degree by taking the courses he took in high school. I guess I shouldn't be surprised that he didn't want to endure any more, but it makes me very sad to think of what we all lose when we do this to such a child.

Eric's only scholarship was a one-time $2,000 award from the National Merit Scholarship Foundation. We were told that the fact that he was not valedictorian weighs heavily against him in awarding merit money. He wouldn't have received the $2,000 except for a strange happening. Since Eric had scored 800 on the SAT-M at age twelve, he was advised not to retake the SAT-M by the Educational Testing Service. Thereafter, when he took the other parts of the test, his SAT-M score was reported as 200. It was strange to see the 800 followed by a row of 200's. At any rate, his guidance counselor called the National Merit Scholarship Foundation to inquire about which scores to report. He was told that Eric would have to retake the entire exam, that they wouldn't accept a score that old. He did this in early November 1987, and scored another 800 in math plus 710 verbal. In early February he received a letter from the National Merit Scholarship Foundation telling him that he had not qualified for finalist because of his low math score. I called them and learned that the Educational Testing Service had never reported his November scores and they had only the 200. I subsequently learned that the colleges to which he had applied had not received his scores either nor had the committee that was considering him as a Presidential Scholar. I think it was finally straightened out.

As I mentioned before, Eric is a very private person. One of his teachers said that Eric had more reasons to brag than any kid he knew, but he never said a word. He attended the Biology Olympics at a local college during his senior year, and when I asked him how the team did, he said, "Fine." He never told me that he had received an individual first place for an unprecedented 100 percent in the area of genetics. I read it in the newspaper, in an article the district published.

I don't know if we would fight the battle again. I don't think we had much choice with Eric. He needed our support because he was miserable at school, at least in the elementary grades. We did keep him out of most of the inappropriate classes the district tried to force on him. He spent four and a half years in math classes out of the thirteen that he attended school. He had tutors who really challenged and valued him; he had an exceptional math teacher in the CCAC program; he had some teachers in the district who appreciated and encouraged him; the author of the *Elements of Mathematics Program* was wonderful to him and it was that program more than any other that stretched his mind; and, above all, he had his brother, Doug, who encouraged and challenged and complemented him. The two of them were an amazing team with Doug explaining verbally and Eric providing the intuition. There has to be a better way than legal battles; they take too long. The child does not stand still. We should never have had to do any of this; Eric should have been valued.

To other parents, I say never give up. Refuse to accept what you know is wrong for your child. Your child has no one but you to defend him or her. The best way I know to achieve progress would be for parents to band together and demand a change. The politicians and the bureaucracy won't initiate a thing and the teacher's union will protect the teachers. I think we live in a strange world, one in which we want all kinds of scientific and medical breakthroughs but one in which most people are jealous and resentful of providing opportunities for the very children who can some day make these breakthroughs.

Update

Our sons have achieved in spite of the system, not because of it. Doug graduated from Carnegie Mellon University with two bachelor of science degrees and university honors in mathematics and electrical and computer engineering. He received a full-funding scholarship to a seven-year M.D./Ph.D. program at Baylor College of Medicine in Houston. He wants to do medical research. Eric has been carrying a heavy load at Princeton and getting A's as usual; he has been accepted to Princeton's Woodrow Wilson School of Public and International Affairs where he will continue in economics plus add politics and government. We are not pleased that his fourteen college math courses have led nowhere. Mathematicians are in short supply.

Lauren took Calculus I at Carnegie Mellon and received an A. She is now in eleventh grade, just completed Calculus II at CMU and has no math course for her final year of high school. Now, what should we do about that?

The Ferguson Family

The Ferguson family has many interests and hobbies. Sally is a housewife, substitute teacher, and also works in home sales for a national cosmetic firm. She holds an undergraduate degree from Mansfield University, Mansfield, Pennsylvania. She has won several singing awards, including first place in the National Grange Family Competition, and has made an album with her sisters. Bob teaches math and is a certified program specialist in gifted education. He received both his undergraduate and graduate degrees from Mansfield University. Sally and Bob are active in civic and church activities and have held elected positions in many organizations. Bob is founder and director of the oldest chess camp in the United States, and has received several awards for chess.

Their sons, Ryan and Rob, attended a private school for two years and then were home schooled for two years before entering public school. Ryan, who is currently in the eighth grade, was identified as gifted upon entering the public schools. Rob, a high school freshman, is dyslexic although he has performance scores in the gifted range on intelligence tests. The boys have won a wide range of awards in chess, have many hobbies, and are active in their church youth groups.

As a family, they enjoy chess activities, reading (together and separately), and traveling. They have journeyed through much of the United States and many European countries.

Checkmate

In order to develop an appropriate individual educational plan (IEP) for Ryan after he was identified as gifted, we believed it was necessary to consider his specific needs, strengths, and interests, as well as our concerns as parents. Upon arriving at the meeting to discuss the IEP, we were given a prewritten document. We felt it was inappropriate to hand out a completed IEP at the beginning of the planning meeting. We also believed it imperative to include the insights of the individuals who knew him best to develop an appropriate IEP, and this should be the outcome of the IEP meeting. Parents' suggestions should not be disregarded just to make the process faster and easier for the school district staff.

One and a half pages of objectives, instructional methods, and materials seem insufficient to describe what will happen during 1,440 class periods. Will any textbooks be used in the interdisciplinary course which incorporates spelling, English, reading, and social studies? We wanted more details. As his parents, we believe that educational goals and objectives should be written specifically enough to permit assessment of what is accomplished. Unless the goals are measurable, we did not consider them adequate. Behavioral objectives should quantify and qualify what, when, where, and how they are to be accomplished. Short term objectives such as "participate in the development of . . . listening skills" did not tell what would be done, what specific resources would be used, or how they would be accomplished. As a teacher, I had seen IEP objectives listed this way before and had seen the negative consequences. Usually nothing tangible happened.

We itemized Ryan's needs as follows: cultivate the art of listening; develop analytical and creative thinking skills;

improve organization skills and self-motivation; enhance self-esteem; continue in the advanced math program; develop leadership skills; and learn to cope with peer pressure. Ryan's interest areas were: math and science; chess; collecting coins, baseball cards, and stamps; reading; music; and history.

Ryan hates English and spelling and is not fond of the traditional reading program at school. We felt that creating an IEP around his least favorite subjects was inappropriate, especially when it excluded his needs, strengths, and interests. We personally believed that Ryan's interests should be used as vehicles to develop his skills because this is a more palatable approach.

We also believed the district's commitment to the intellectually gifted should be equal to that for the psychomotor gifted as evidenced by athletics and other such programs. Why is discrimination between types of giftedness so extreme?

Chess, as Ryan's major interest area, should be specifically included in the IEP to foster growth in thinking skills, interpersonal relationships, and self-esteem. We disagreed with the administrator who stated that "chess does not appear to be a major issue."

In the Prehearing Conference Report, it was stated: "The district does not believe *Odyssey of the Mind* to be a necessary or appropriate program to be included in the Gifted IEP." Why had it been included for Ryan for so many years, if it was inappropriate? We believed this action discriminated against Ryan's needs and interests and against all others who were similarly deprived by the district. The intent appeared to be to reduce money for the intellectually gifted.

As a teacher in the system, I was more aware of the tactics used by administrators to postpone decisions. In a previous incident in which I was involved on behalf of a pupil, the school district was able to postpone the student's due process hearing for nearly nine months; by then he had graduated. I, therefore, established our expectations at the IEP conference and immediately scheduled a prehearing conference, which was held on June 1, 1989. The administrators at the prehearing conference conveniently could not find the necessary form for us to sign, a strategy that has been used with other less knowledgeable parents. The form was typed by the secretary the next day, and my wife and I responded on June 3, 1989. The district never forwarded the Prehearing Conference Report to anyone, so on July 14, 1989, and on ten other dates throughout July and August, I called the Right to Education Office to speak to someone to discuss our problems. We never sought legal counsel to attempt to expedite closure.

Confronting my superiors during the hearing and having to point out their inconsistencies became quite stressful. I have to work for these people every day, and unfortunately, their track record on forgiving and forgetting is quite poor. The entire due process hearing was stressful because of the formality of it all. We were unable to express our feelings adequately within the constraints of this formal structure.

Since I had never attended a hearing before, I was at quite a disadvantage in acting as my own counsel. The format of the hearing seemed confusing and illogical. We had a difficult time following the line of questioning and cross-examination procedure. We thought we were permitted to ask all of our questions during our cross-examination. Being corrected repeatedly made it very difficult to remember which questions we had asked.

The Right to Education Office in our state capital was excellent in providing written materials and answers to our questions. I consulted with the local hearing officer who gave me some good guidelines for preparing for the due proc-

ess hearing. The administrators for the district were the
greatest obstacle to resolving problems. The administrators
individually had given us contradictory answers; however,
they had an opportunity to band together and plan their
strategy and testimony prior to the hearing. Their responses
were quite different from their original statements.

The major accomplishment of our due process hearing
was that our son was granted the opportunity to pursue a
mentorship study with the resident chess master during his
study halls. This established a precedent. Chess has been
used in other gifted programs to develop thinking skills and
was formerly included in our district; however, our district
cut the budget and staff for the gifted in 1987 and put an
end to chess. I thought it was odd that the district would
spend so much money to fight against something that would
cost them nothing. The master had been offered to the district at no charge for up to twenty hours per week. There
were no other significant outcomes.

We were very pleased that chess was eventually included,
but we were not successful in continuing *Odyssey of the
Mind* as part of Ryan's IEP. We also felt his educational needs
and the provisions for meeting those needs should have been
written out in some detail. No written changes were provided, although some minor adaptions were made.

I would fight the battle again; it was definitely worth the
time and effort. I learned a great deal from the experience
and feel that I am now better equipped to help others who
are having similar problems.

I believe every parent has the duty to stay informed about
educational issues. The parent should not view his or her
request for a due process hearing as a burden to the district.
Parents know a child better than the educational experts
who spend an hour or two testing and determining present
levels of education. Parents must exert their influence, if

there is to be positive change in the field of education. If parents do not have an attorney and are uncertain about how to proceed, they should contact a hearing officer or their state office for guidance. I would recommend that most individuals consider trying the Special Education Mediation Services prior to scheduling a due process hearing, if such a service is available in their state. I would recommend others consult with legal counsel and/or discuss in detail all aspects of the hearing process with a hearing officer prior to attempting to act as their own counsel.

If you will permit a slight digression, I will use a simple analogy. Baking soda has been used by many over the years to clean their teeth, and it works reasonably well. However, most youngsters do not find it palatable and would prefer to use something more colorful, interesting, and tasty — such as a popular toothpaste. If an individual will brush longer and more often with this toothpaste than with baking soda, then research will tell us that he will have fewer cavities. The same holds true in education. We need to use Ryan's interest areas to insure that he will "brush longer" so he will learn more from the experience. Chess is a vehicle in which Ryan has considerable interest and it can be used in a variety of ways to provide for his needs.

Chess, as a vehicle for teaching thinking skills, is currently being used in seventeen countries around the world as a part of the curriculum. In the June 1988 issue of *Reader's Digest*, Jo Coudert tells how chess has helped to meet the needs of students in East Harlem. Research on five continents has verified that chess is a superior vehicle for developing thinking and problem solving skills. My son would rather use chess than baking soda any day.

As I write this, Ryan is laboring over a grammar lesson. This brings to mind the hundreds of research studies that have attempted to prove that teaching grammar helps pupils improve their communication skills. Of course, none of them have been able to prove this, and in several cases the researchers have proven that instruction in grammar has a negative effect upon communication skills. But we still insist on doing this to kids, even as a part of the gifted program, because we've always done it. Why should this be part of a gifted program? Do you really stop and ask yourself am I using a noun substantive or a gerundive correctly? Most kids find this worse than brushing with baking soda, and so does Ryan. He loathes spelling and English, and yet this is what he is offered in his IEP as being appropriate. He does not desire a generic gifted program; he wants his needs and interests met. We agree with him.

The Rankin Family

In the Rankin family of Sevierville, Tennessee, both parents are college graduates with additional hours toward master's degrees. Wendy, the mother, currently takes graduate classes in gifted education. In addition to working part time in the family business, she actively advises parents who face similar difficulties with school systems, and makes presentations on due process to parent groups and at state and national conferences.

David, the father, works full time (and then some) in the printing company he started ten years ago. He is actively involved in church-related projects, enjoys leisure reading and time with the family, and does his own laundry!

Scott, in the ninth grade, was a national finalist in the Duke University Talent Identification Program and attends summer classes at Duke each year. Although his experience at middle school was unchallenging, he hopes for a stimulating environment in high school. Scott enjoys piano, plays tenor saxophone in the senior high band, and is a technician in the drama club. Scott is also very active in church youth activities, reads extensively and does his own laundry.

Chaney, in seventh grade, attends an excellent public elementary school in a neighboring town. She will have an accelerated language arts program and pre-algebra, and will earn high school credits. Her regular classroom curriculum is compacted, freeing her to interact with an excellent teacher of gifted students. Chaney dances and plays the piano and drums, but her main interests are reading, creative writing, and her extensive paperdoll collection. She, too, achieved national recognition in the 1991 Duke University Talent Identification Program, and plans to attend the summer programs.

Due Process as a Siege!
Advice to Future Combatants

Six years of frustration on our part and noncompliance on the part of the school system preceded our due process hearing. Needless to say, one doesn't just "go due process" over a single issue without some degree of prior difficulty with the system and/or its personnel. We had been trying to modify our son's regular classroom curriculum for five years. We had finally given up, and with the approval of the current superintendent, had placed our children in a struggling private school. When we left the public system for the private school, we took several of the brighter students with us. For the one semester that we were enrolled in the private option, that student body boasted the highest percentage of identified gifted students in one building in the county. This situation may have contributed to the fact that the public system then created a special accelerated class as a pilot program in the building we had just left. In an unrelated move, the system also had placed this building in a different school zone, making access to the special program selective. The private option turned out to be fraught with its own internal difficulties, and we decided to home school until the following fall.

Enrollment in that private option went from 26 students prior to our involvement, 60 during our involvement, and 36 immediately following our withdrawal. It now boasts an enrollment of 17 students. I mention this to demonstrate that we were not the only ones to experiment and reject this option.

The due process hearing came about when we decided to reenroll our daughter in the school with the pilot accelerated program. Our son was too old for such an option. Because the school was zoned, we were denied access to the program. It was our contention that the least restrictive environment for our daughter would be with her chronological peers who would be accelerated as she had been through her home school opportunities.

Although the specific issue of the hearing was placement in a special class within a zoned school, the chronic issue was modification of our children's regular classroom curriculum to meet their needs and compliance with state guidelines for handicapped/exceptional students. I spent years in battle with the principal of this school who felt that his interpretation of appropriate education for gifted children should prevail over any state laws. Unfortunately it took me years to discover that he was not the final authority on such matters. I went through all the proper channels prior to filing for due process: teacher conferences, multidisciplinary team meetings, a hearing with the superintendent, and a hearing with the school board. It was not until I decided that they just couldn't keep our younger child out of this accelerated class after denying our older child acceleration for six years that we filed for due process.

Once we requested this hearing, I became concerned that my lack of expertise on due process would prevent me from being successful. I started making phone calls all over the state for help in the formalities of due process. I was told by the system that an agency called Effective Advocacy for Children with Handicaps (EACH) was available to advise me. EACH declined to help on the grounds that the hearing involved a gifted child and their funding was from the national level which did not identify gifted as handicapped. This incident bears looking into because this state organization should be helping all state identified handicapped students!

I finally contacted two school psychologists who were former due process hearing officers who agreed to assist us. We spent several hours discussing the predicament, and in the course of discussion I learned that most of the issues which I had been battling over were simple rights already afforded our children by the state rules and regulations! In other words, I had spent six years trying unsuccessfully to get a principal to obey a twelve-year-old law! It was at this point that the psychologists agreed to be our consultants and advised us to consider also hiring an attorney for the hearing. This would have meant paying the attorney as well as the consultants by the hour and the attorney would have to be briefed by the consultants every step of the way. We hoped that the cost of the hearing would be reimbursed by the system since many areas of noncompliance were established; and we didn't want to burden the system with added legal fees. Based on these concerns, we decided to engage the consultants alone; this ended up being a costly decision.

We met with the representatives of the school system, our consultants and a state department arbitrator prior to the hearing in order to settle the dispute. It was at this point that we locked into our five issues.

We listed the following points to the due process hearing officer:

1. Appropriate placement of the gifted child within the system
2. Reimbursement of private school tuition paid by parents on the grounds that the superintendent approved of private option as only alternative
3. Correction or rewriting of Individualized Education Plan (IEP) for current year
4. Parent reimbursement for hearing expense
5. Temporary placement pending final order

This move took the system by surprise as they were expecting a zoning issue as the sole point of contention. They never accepted that prior issues of noncompliance or improper handling of my children should have been a part of the hearing. They publicized the hearing as strictly a zoning issue because it was becoming evident that the system was in trouble over these other issues.

Outcome

1. *Appropriate placement of the gifted child.* Five days before the hearing the school system canceled the special class, explaining to the eighty parents involved that things were rocking right along until the Rankins filed for due process. Enter community animosity. Not only that, but how can a due process hearing officer place a child in a program that does not exist? To this day the system contends to themselves and the public that they won the hearing because the child did not break the zone. They never mention that they canceled the class because they knew they couldn't prevail. Nor do many people know that ten days after the hearing they reinstated the acceleration under a new process, thus appeasing the parents. So we entered the hearing knowing that our daughter would not be placed in the special program which no longer existed. But our very clever and knowledgeable consultants had worded point numer one in such a way that we prevailed anyway since her placement was appropriate to the remaining options.

2. *Reimbursement of private school tuition.* Evidence from the testimony suggested that we were entitled to reimbursement for the private schooling had it been an appropriate placement. Once we withdrew from that option then we determined that it was not an appropriate placement, and therefore were not awarded reimbursement. We made our point about the superintendent encouraging the placement, but we lost the money because the placement was not a good option.

3. *Correction of the IEP.* We prevailed and our poor seven-year-old daughter spent two weeks being assessed and tested right out of second grade.

4. *Parent reimbursement for hearing expenses.* We were awarded fees which the system later appealed and won because, although we deserved the reimbursement, the law states that it be for lawyer's fees and we had used consultants instead. Had we paid a lawyer $80.00 per hour to watch the proceedings it would have cost the system double, but the system would have paid rather than us.

5. *Temporary placement.* Our daughter was temporarily placed at a school within her zone and an appropriate IEP was created at our expense since it was our consultant who understood what an appropriate IEP should look like.

So on paper we prevailed on four of the five points, but in the newspaper and the community we lost because our daughter did not cross the zone. Ironically, I have a list of many children who have since crossed the zone for a variety of reasons, none of which were academic and many of which were suspect. So who said life was fair?

The real or long term outcome of our suit has nothing to do with the original issues; many changes resulted from the hearing. The concept of modifying classroom curriculum is at least acknowledged as appropriate, even if it is done with considerable stress to the child. I look back at our hearing as a series of tragic, sad circumstances much of which stemmed from a stubborn, ill-informed building principal and timing. My children both suffered deeply as did the entire family but none as much as my older son. He has yet to have an appropriate education in this county. Things are much better for his sister but only because she is fortunate enough to be under the wing of a trained teacher of gifted education. They have learned how to question and how to stand up for their rights, but there is little comfort in the short run in such a lesson.

The greatest hurdle we faced during the hearing was protecting our children from system personnel determined to prove us wrong through our children. The system was very adept at coloring the picture and there is little empathy for the plight of gifted children in the community anyway. People rely on old myths and assumptions of elitism rather than understanding that there could possibly be a hardship for bright kids.

A significant portion of testimony was stricken from the records because it was taken over the phone from a teacher who had since moved. This testimony was to be confirmed in writing by the court reporter, but the system neglected to provide the court reporter with the teacher's current address and phone number. That was frustrating for me because the testimony was particularly damaging for the system.

We were supported incognito by many system personnel who knew of the injustices which we had endured. We were gratified by the large show of support from many teachers but saddened by the ones who were intimidated by being associated with us, the enemy.

Advice to Others

From the situation that I, as a parent of gifted children, had to experience to receive a due process hearing, I feel compelled to give advice to others who may be faced with similar circumstances. Based on the situation we experienced, here are some ways to document and collect evidence, expenses you may be faced with, and the rewards you may gain.

Remember those casual conversations with your child's teacher while chaperoning a field trip or in the doorway of the classroom? Picture yourself repeating one of these conversations under oath while testifying in a due process hearing! How many of these casual exchanges influenced the formation of your child's program? How much of the information obtained in such a casual manner was either false or at the very least misleading? Regular classroom teachers are not experts on state rules and regulations, nor should they be. They are often victims of tradition which can turn them into victims of a due process hearing. I'll never forget the look on the face of a teacher, who was also a friend, when she realized that testifying was putting herself in danger with her superiors. Even worse was the look on another's face when she chose job security and system loyalty over principle.

As I look back on the years leading up to our due process experience, I now realize that much of the noncompliance surrounding services for my two children was promoted by my not following a simple rule: Ask your question in writing and get your answer in writing. When a person has to put his or her answer in writing with a signature affixed, that person usually takes great care to be sure that the answer is not only accurate but within state guidelines. This simple process can promote change in policy. Wrong as it may be, you must take responsibility for allowing the system to disregard rules and regulations in favor of convenience, cost and/or tradition.

Second, once you have an answer in writing, you have evidence. Keep a paper trail! I was able to reconstruct evidence of crucial conversations because I had referred to them in letters which I had kept copies. Even having discussed incidents in the hall with other teachers or mothers was admissible evidence. Had I kept a log of every discussion relating to my children's schooling, I could have tripled evidence of noncompliance.

This brings us to the issue of recognizing noncompliance when it occurs. If you don't have a copy of the relevant state rules and regulations, how do you know that your system is following minimum requirements? If your child's gifted pull-out class is being held in the broom closet or worse yet, outside on the patio, "weather permitting," are they being served in facilities according to state rules? Citing noncompliance in the handling of your child's services allows you to prevail, at least on those issues.

If you are going to take an issue to the due process stage, be careful to list all points of contention separately in order to increase the likelihood of prevailing. Your main problem may not be decided in your favor, but you can be sure that secondary issues of noncompliance will be.

One issue for our hearing was an accelerated class in a zoned school. As mentioned earlier, five days before the hearing, the system canceled the class. How could the hearing officer place us in a nonexistent class? Of course we didn't prevail on that issue. Fortunately, other points were easy wins because the system was negligent in handling our children. What will never go on record is the fact that ten days after the hearing, the system quietly reinstituted the acceleration without calling it a special class.

Be prepared for a long siege if you are considering due process. In addition to the hearing itself, which in our case lasted well beyond midnight, it was **months** before the final results came through. By then our child was already settled and further adjustments in her program could have been counterproductive.

You may not be able to count on confidentiality. As a matter of fact, if you choose to keep the hearing closed, you may be giving the system control over what information leaks and what doesn't. Because our controversy centered around an accelerated class involving more than eighty children, it was to the system's advantage to placate those parents by placing the blame on us. Rather than justify having canceled this class five days before the hearing because they knew that by law they couldn't deny our child access to it, they told the parent that "Everything was rocking along just fine until the Rankins filed due process." In other words, they could have gotten away with serving this select few group of children as long as those excluded hadn't complained. I couldn't even volunteer in the school clinic without facing the resentment of other parents who claimed "Everybody's upset with you, why don't you put your children in a private school or something?" We had become public enemy number one!

My two bright children seemed to be a burden for the community as well as the system. Years earlier the superintendent had suggested over lunch that the system couldn't provide for children with needs such as mine and that I should save them by going to a local private school. I later learned that this advice could be considered system endorsement for a placement at the expense of the system! When the superintendent didn't deny the conversation, the hearing officer considered reimbursement for us for our brief encounter with the private school. However, since the children reentered public schools once the accelerated class became available, I thereby determined that the private school placement was inappropriate and not deserving of reimbursement. I guess the important lesson here is that lunch conversations can be considered official if a change of program results from them. Jot down casual conversations and stick them in a file in case they become crucial evidence in a hearing.

Be aware of the hidden costs of a due process hearing. Our telephone bill was in the hundreds of dollars and not even listed as an expense. We were fortunate enough to have used two education consultants who happened to be school psychologists and former due process hearing officers. What could have been better than to be aided by knowledgeable, sympathetic, experienced consultants? Guess what? Had we allowed these consultants to hire lawyers, the bill would have doubled and the lawyers would have been window-dressers, but the state law provides reimbursement for lawyer's fees only, and the school system would have had to foot the bill rather than us! We had to foot our share of a bill for fighting an appeal by the system which cost the system more than paying our bill would have.

Understand that people are uncomfortable with the concept of gifted and cannot see such a child as a victim. The worst example of sabotage involved the packets that I was instructed to prepare for the actual hearing. I photocopied and highlighted page after page of documents, letters, and notes from teachers, making sure that all critical points were immediately obvious. I duplicated these packets for all participants of the hearing and turned them over to the system. Because I was working off my own packet when we verified that all documents were submitted, I didn't discover until weeks later that the system had recopied my packets using a dismal machine which left much to the imagination. When rephotocopied my yellow highlighter turned black and obscured what it was supposed to be highlighting! So much for clear documentation.

Once the dust had cleared, I was asked to write about the hearing for a national newsletter. I would begin to tell my story and become so outraged at the variety of injustices, that I could not coherently put the story to paper. It wasn't until I began to give pointers to other parents and then to make presentations to groups on how to go about preparing for a due process hearing that I could begin to sort out the emotions from the useful skills I had acquired. I still find it difficult to bypass the horror stories!

Believe it or not, there are bright moments that make it all worthwhile. We learned who our real friends were and, as hurtful a process as that was, it has its rewards. We discovered allies within the system. We continue to get referrals of parents in distress from the most unlikely sources. We get phone calls from teachers reporting other issues of noncompliance. We see marked improvement in the delivery of service systemwide as a result of the turmoil. All of the appropriate school personnel actually show up now for our Multipledisciplinary-Team meetings! New Individualized Education Plan (IEP) forms actually use words such as compacting, acceleration, and enrichment! One administrator has spoken of a meeting where the decision to comply with a certain regulation was made "in case the Rankins get wind of the issue." I get real answers to my questions, and most of them are within the rules and regulations. Skills which I developed during this situation are useful to everyday life. I learned to live with rumors and to excuse people who didn't know the whole story. I know how to get help and how to help others. The most important outcome of the entire experience is that the children learned how to stand up for what they believe in, even under extreme duress. I remember a parent saying in church one day, "Oh, I could never ask my daughter to be different, even though I know she wants and needs this accelerated program." Well, what is she going to do when the issues of being like everyone else include cheating, drugs, or worse? At least my children know what priority to place on their values.

Would we do it over again, now that we know what can happen? Before answering that, let me tell you the bottom line. No matter what the laws say, no matter how much you know, and no matter how "good" the system is that you are in, if the regular classroom teacher doesn't understand gifted issues or, worse yet, doesn't care, you've got trouble. You start over each and every year. Due process is an empty victory without a well-trained, cooperative, and empathic teacher. Even worse, if your system is truly inept in the area of gifted, as well as easily intimidated, you can find yourself being the expert and unintentionally implementing a program that is not in the best interest of your child. So, first and foremost, advocate for enlightenment of the teachers and the system.

If we had it to do over again, would we? Yes. As painful as it was, we are stronger and better off for having done it. The system learned and grew from the ordeal. Things are better up to a point. And there is nothing sweeter than sitting in a parent meeting, listening to the president say "If it weren't for the Rankins . . ."

The Andrews Family

Carolyn and Andy Andrews have three children and live in Oliver Springs, Tennessee. Ned was born in 1980; John in 1983; and Gary in 1988. Ned and John were identified as gifted at ages four and five, respectively.

Carolyn has been a homemaker since Ned's birth. Andy is a development engineer at Oak Ridge National Laboratory in Oak Ridge, Tennessee. The Andrews live in a county where opposition to tax increases is fierce. From time to time they consider moving to an area where education gets more financial respect. Meanwhile, Carolyn tries to keep abreast of local school developments by attending school board meetings. Helping to form a local parent association for gifted and talented education is an idea she is giving consideration at this time.

"I Have Drunk From Many Wells
I Did Not Dig"

I first encountered this quotation years ago during one of the annual financial campaigns of my college alma mater. In the spring of 1990 I became acutely aware of how relevant the quotation was for my husband and me in our battle to meet the educational needs of our intellectually gifted children. For this and other reasons I am eager to share our story.

The legal protection accorded gifted students is the result of contributions and struggles of countless unnamed individuals. Many other individuals have struggled desperately to reap what is guaranteed by law and, even more poignantly, to *know* what is guaranteed by law. "Knowing" was a big obstacle for our family, and it is there that our story begins. Perhaps our story will be a well from which other families may drink.

Our first child, now a ten-year-old, is extremely precocious, though we did not realize it at the time. A neighbor, who was a fourth grade teacher, met Ned when he was twelve months old. Visit after visit, she continued to insist that he was extremely intelligent and unusual for his age. Because he was our first child, we had no point of reference and we took the neighbor's comments lightly.

As time wore on and as we started paying attention to the intellectual capacity of other children Ned's age, we began to realize that our teacher friend was not simply giving idle praise regarding this mental ability. Others were noticing him, sometimes in ways that have proven to be detrimental. The most vivid example I can remember is the time a couple seriously suggested, in front of this child who was only two years old but who could understand the entire meaning of the conversation, that he be put on the television show,

"That's Incredible!" (Incidentally, we did not pursue this suggestion.) From very early on, this child had a burden of proving himself.

When Ned was about two and a half years old, I began wondering if there were any federal or state programs available for intellectually superior children. I simply did not know; but it stood to reason that if there were programs for children who had learning problems, there should be something available for children like him. I was having difficulty "keeping up" with his insatiable curiosity and felt that I did not have the training to meet his needs at what seemed to be a period of readiness. I felt inadequate; I needed help.

I contacted our local education agency (LEA), our county school system. I spoke with the school psychologist and discussed my concerns and questions with her. She did not know if anything was available, but she promised to find out. She investigated and learned that until a child was four years old nothing could be provided by the LEA. We agreed that I would contact her when Ned reached his fourth birthday and that he would then be tested. The initial encounter with the system and the school psychologist was extremely positive. Though our relationship has been strained over the years by my exercising our rights to compliance and due process, I still feel an indebtedness to this person for her sensitivity to our child's needs.

In the meantime, an acquaintance, who would later become a friend, noticed Ned's ability. A seasoned teacher of the gifted, she approached me and asked if I realized that he had special abilities and needs. I told her that I had contacted our LEA and that I was waiting for his fourth birthday so that he could be evaluated. She provided me with lists of enrichment materials I might wish to use to help meet his needs. She also told me about a support group that I might wish to join. This group, a local arm of the Tennessee Association for the Gifted, would prove to be very helpful to me in later struggles. I cannot overemphasize the importance of listening to even casual suggestions offered by others experienced in the area of gifted education.

Shortly after Ned's fourth birthday, he was tested and certified as intellectually gifted. The LEA supervisor of special education admitted that the system was "plowing new ground" with this child, for never before had the LEA been asked to serve an intellectually gifted preschooler. At no point did the system try to shirk its responsibility. The problem was not "whether" to do it; it was "how" to do it. The school psychologist suggested that we consider a Montessori school and also a public preschool in a nearby city for placement. However, we had another small child by that time; and the thought of making two trips per day to transport the older child to school — even though I would be reimbursed for the transportation — was not an inviting one.

In my search to decide what I might suggest to the LEA as a way to meet Ned's needs, I took a step that would prove to be helpful to me in subsequent struggles. I contacted the head of the department of special education at the University of Tennessee and told him about our child. I asked for suggestions. I even had copies of Ned's test scores and psychological assessment sent to him. My contact with him would become helpful to me on numerous occasions in years to come.

I suggested to the LEA that we consider letting Ned spend part of the day at the local elementary school in a special program which we could devise for him. His schedule was arranged so that he could ride the bus to school, spend part of the morning with the kindergarten class in socialization and physical education activities, and then spend time each day with the special education teacher. I would then pick him up shortly before lunch.

Interestingly, when I contacted the principal of our home district school to arrange a time to discuss with him Ned's proposed schedule, he informed me that Ned would have to go to another elementary school — not his. It was clear that this unusual situation was something he did not care to deal with. Something told me not to take "no" for an answer. I pursued the matter, and Ned was placed at this school.

Although convenient for me, this arrangement did not meet Ned's needs. However, the kindergarten teacher, in particular, was excellent. She took it upon herself to obtain materials of special interest to Ned from other classrooms and was extremely flexible in dealing with his age in relation to her other students.

It was obvious that Ned needed to be in an environment where the curriculum could naturally grow with his needs. Also, it was important that he be with chronological age peers. However, by the time this became evident, the LEA was seemingly comfortable with trying to meet Ned's needs within the system. The status quo was financially attractive.

In the spring I took it upon myself to visit and observe many alternative environments. After thorough study, I decided that the Montessori school in the nearby city, initially suggested by the school psychologist, would best meet his needs. I prepared a booklet that listed what I considered to be Ned's needs and described how the Montessori environment would meet them. The kindergarten teacher and the school psychologist were in full agreement with me on this matter, and we convinced the system that there should be a change in placement. The system tried to discourage us by making an issue of whether or not the school was state approved. As it turned out, this criterion did not have to be met by a preschool program in order for the LEA to obtain state funds.

I do not believe that the system was actually hesitant to do what was in Ned's best interest, but I do believe that on this and many occasions to follow that it often responded with answers and arguments based on ignorance. Often it reacted negatively to requests simply out of fear of being guilty of misappropriation of funds. Had I not been tenacious and refused to take "no" for an answer, many opportunities would have been denied Ned.

Ned had a highly beneficial year at the Montessori school. (For parents of preschoolers who are interested in Montessori education, I should warn that anyone can claim to run a Montessori school. You must carefully evaluate the program to determine the quality of the school.) The year provided no headaches to the system, which agreed to send Ned there for the next academic year also. Had the LEA wished to be stingy with its funds, it could have insisted that Ned enter public school at this time. This next year was to be his kindergarten year, and kindergarten was provided as a formal program by the system. However, the LEA recognized that Ned had begun a program that was highly beneficial to him; and I believe that it also recognized that it was in his best interest to continue with this program. The system was also well aware that I would have argued vigorously against a change in placement.

As Ned's second year at the Montessori school drew to a close, placement again became an issue. The Montessori school did not have a junior program. That spring I began a search for what I believed to be the most appropriate environment for his first-grade year. Talks with the LEA school psychologist resulted in a suggestion that Ned be placed at a specific elementary school that had a higher census of children whose ability levels more closely approximated his. This school was not Ned's home school but was within the system.

I visited and observed this school and talked with all of the first-grade teachers. One teacher in particular seemed to truly understand the dilemmas facing intellectually gifted children, so I decided that I would request that she be the teacher to serve Ned. Because Ned would be a "new kid" in this school the next fall, I arranged for him to spend a day that spring with this teacher and her first graders.

The teacher, a highly experienced educator with a master's degree in special education, took me aside at the end of the day of Ned's visit. Earnestly and with great concern, she said that Ned would be out of place at this school and that I should consider sending him to a private school that could progress with him at a faster rate. She said that if we did not wish to send him to a private school, we should at least place him directly in the second grade in public school the following fall. She stressed that he already knew everything that those children were now doing at the end of the year. She said that he would probably need to "skip" another grade somewhere down the line and that when he became a fifth grader we should look into sending him to a specific local college preparatory school that serves grades five through twelve.

This teacher had displayed much insight into the needs of special children, and I was impressed by her comments. In retrospect, I probably should have engaged her help in requesting that the LEA meet Ned's needs outside the system — just as I had engaged the help of the kindergarten teacher two years previously. However, I did not. I don't know why. After much deliberation, I decided that I still wanted Ned to be a first grader with this teacher. I was strongly opposed to allowing him to "skip" a grade, for I felt that because he was a boy and because his social skills among children were below average, he should be with his chronological age peers.

At this time, I began to have a conflict with the LEA. Talks with the school psychologist became strained at this point, for she also recommended strongly that Ned be placed directly in second grade. She pointed out that the first grade teacher had said that physically Ned would "fit in" with those rising second graders.

I stood firm. I wanted him in first grade for socialization reasons. I made my stand known to the supervisor of special education, who then produced a memorandum from the state commission of education. The memorandum stated that "in all cases the determination of whether a pupil is promoted or retained in grade or which class he is assigned to (transition or regular, advanced or basic) is made by appropriate school officials, not parents."

I could not accept this answer. I asked the supervisor of special education to give me the name of the state education agency (SEA) contact person who could confirm this information. By great fortune I eventually spoke with someone in the SEA — not recommended to me, but someone who would help me on numerous occasions throughout the following years both to obtain correct information and to point out to the system that certain answers given me were misleading and/or erroneous. This individual was a compliance officer in the program compliance administration.

The compliance officer explained that the memorandum shown to me did not apply to special education students. The memorandum had come about, in part, in response to efforts by parents of regular education students who wished to retain their children so they would have one more year of eligibility to play sports.

She explained that with special education students it was the duty of the multidisciplinary team (M-Team) to make the decision regarding grade placement. She made it clear that the parent was part of this M-Team. Although I had, in the past, voiced my opinion and struggled to obtain what I felt was in Ned's best interest, it was not until this time that I fully realized the power the parent has in making decisions regarding the child's education. The compliance officer suggested that I speak with the SEA's director of talented and gifted regarding the information that had been given me. The director was a dedicated advocate. She suggested resource books for me to read, and she made me aware that she was available to be of help in seeing that the needs of the child were met. I was to feel free to call upon her at any time.

The school year ended before any decisions were made regarding the following academic year for Ned. Upon several occasions in the early summer I verbally requested that the system meet with me to make plans for the fall, but I was constantly put off. Tired with the delay, I once again contacted the compliance officer. She guided me in the writing of a letter requesting an M-Team meeting, which the system would be unable to ignore. In retrospect, I wonder why I did not think of this myself. Parents are so unaware of their rights, and my ignorance at this time underscores the importance of not being hesitant to seek out answers from people who are in a position to know.

The M-Team meeting was granted. I knew that the system was going to push for Ned's "skipping" a grade, and I knew that I wanted much more for Ned than the system would offer on its own. I contacted the SEA's director of talented and gifted and asked if she would be able to attend the meeting. Though the meeting was more than three hours in driving time from her office, she immediately agreed to put it on her calendar. I was astonished by how willing she was to fulfill what I considered to be a monumental request. She responded, matter of factly, that this was her job.

I had made some of my ideas known to the LEA before the meeting, and I had already been told by more than one system official that the system was required to provide only a "minimum, not a maximum, program." Sidetracked by this response, I contacted several individuals. My intent was to learn of several programs made available in different parts of the country and to be able to argue that what I was requesting was not a maximum program.

In my search, I learned much about what was being done elsewhere for the gifted. Equally interesting were responses to what I had been told by the system. A former president of the Tennessee Association for the Gifted was thoroughly disgusted. She said that the system must define the child's characteristics and needs and meet them, this being the "minimum" it must do. She stated to me emphatically that the individuals who had drawn the interpretation provided me were "showing their ignorance."

The meeting was held, and the system had many individuals present. We were not informed of who would be in attendance; and this procedural violation — though at the time I didn't know it was a violaltion — would happen again at a critical time years later. Also present were two individuals from our regional SEA office whom I had asked to attend. The meeting lasted more than five hours. The system pushed hard for placing Ned directly in the second grade, and one system official even suggested that Ned be placed directly in the third grade. It was obvious that Ned was not going to fit in anywhere we could place him. With the state director of talented and gifted's professional and eloquent argument, we were able to prevail in our opinion that Ned be a first grader and have program modifications and enrichment when classes would begin in a few weeks.

Most of the suggestions I made regarding program modifications and enrichment were ultimately agreed upon by the

M-Team. One suggestion not supported was my idea that Ned be assigned a mentor in music. The state director of talented and gifted explained that the state did not recognize the visual and performing arts as areas requiring service. At the end of the meeting the services agreed upon were reiterated orally by the SEA's regional right to education coordinator, and we all signed an incomplete IEP. I voiced hesitancy to sign an unfinished document, but I also felt confident that because the right to education coordinator had spelled out the services agreed upon, surely these services — though not yet in writing — would not be in jeopardy. I signed the document with the understanding that I would be provided a complete, typed copy before the start of school.

Though I requested it several times, I was never provided a copy. School started, and the teachers were never informed of the proceedings of the M-Team meeting and the agreements made. Because the M-Team meeting had lasted so long, none of the teachers who would be implementing the IEP were present at the end of the meeting. I had assumed that they would be informed of the decisions. On the third day of school I learned that the regular classroom teacher had been told nothing, so I wrote a letter requesting another M-Team meeting. I informed the system that a due process hearing would be requested if a program were not in place by a given date. This language got things rolling, and Ned's program began immediately.

Upon occasion after this tense period I would have to contact the SEA compliance officer and the regional right to education officer for clarification on certain issues, but there was a relatively long period of smooth sailing. Ned had good teachers who worked with him closely.

At the end of Ned's third grade year, his special education teacher approached me and expressed exasperation at her inability to meet his needs. She wanted to know what I had in mind for him to do the following year. She felt unqualified to do anything more for him. When his younger brother, age five at the time, was tested and also certified as gifted, she bravely pointed out her opinion that the system had done wrong in trying to serve Ned within the system and that she did not want to see the same thing happen with his younger brother. It is not often that a teacher has guts enough to stand up for her beliefs, and I shall always admire this teacher for doing so.

This teacher and I looked into alternative placements, but no overwhelmingly attractive state-approved schools existed nearby. The private school recommended by the first grade teacher was state approved, but it did not begin serving children until the fifth grade. We needed something for the fourth grade year. The special education teacher made it clear that if Ned's needs — and now his brother's — were going to have a chance of being met within the system, another teacher, trained in working with the gifted, would have to be hired by the system. She was trained in working with learning disabled children, and the only reason she was certified to work with gifted was that she was "grandfathered" in by her limited work with a couple of gifted classes a few years previously.

At this point I decided that the LEA's central office needed to know that Ned's needs were not being met. The special education teacher and I met with the supervisor of special education and the school principal to discuss the fact that this teacher believed that a trained teacher needed to be hired. The supervisor and principal listened and lamented that no decisions regarding additional positions for the following year could be made at this time. They also pointed out the lack of space for an additional classroom.

Around this time I informed the supervisor of special education that I would be pursuing alternative placement for

Ned's fifth grade year in a year's time. I reasoned that if alternative placement were to happen, budget planning needed to be done now. The supervisor indicated that enough money would be available should payment of fees be required, but he warned me that only if Ned were "failing or misbehaving" would a change in placement be possible. This statement is another example of what parents might be told by misinformed school officials.

Once again I contacted the compliance officer. I discussed with her the special education teacher's comments and frustrations. Once again, she recommended specific courses of action. Her three recommendations were to (1) petition the system to request that the SEA's new director of talented and gifted help prepare an appropriate individualized education program (IEP) for Ned, (2) encourage the frustrated teacher to take a University of Tennessee summer course in meeting the needs of gifted children, and (3) request that the system hire a local consultant to work with the teacher to devise ways to meet Ned's needs.

This information was presented to the teacher, and she approached the system regarding the first recommendation. A meeting was set up; but to the teacher's and my surprise, the supervisor of special education arranged it to be a county-wide, in-service program on meeting the needs of the gifted in general. No time was set aside to discuss Ned's needs, in particular. After the program, the teacher did approach the director about Ned; but her frustrations were not allayed.

I again approached the supervisor of special education about the possibility of recruiting a teacher trained in working with the gifted. He explained that because of our county's budgeting procedures, there was hardly any chance at all that a new teacher would be hired for the following year. Our county does not usually pass a budget until August, and the supervisor said that not until a budget was passed could another teacher be hired. The opening of school had even been delayed upon occasion in the past because a budget could not be agreed upon before the scheduled opening of school. The supervisor said that he had located good teachers in the past who had taken other positions because they couldn't wait until the start of the school year to know whether or not they would have a job. He also cited the scarcity of special education teachers as a problem.

At this point I decided that I would find the system a candidate trained in working with the gifted. I contacted the special education department of the University of Tennessee and spoke with an instructor of a class of graduate students in gifted education. I discussed our problem with her and she gave me a recommendation, which I pursued. I contacted this individual and asked him if he would be interested in meeting with our system to discuss a job opportunity. He replied that he would, so I relayed this information to our supervisor of special education. The supervisor said that he had no objection to my arranging for this student to meet with Ned's special education teacher. The meeting was held.

Meantime, I spoke with the compliance officer about our system's response that no teacher could be hired until a budget were passed. Again, she offered a concrete suggestion. She recommended that I ask the county to hire the individual I had located as a consultant to help prepare an appropriate IEP for Ned for the fall. I pushed for this, and the individual was hired. However, the consulting work the county asked him to do was to prepare a proposal for a talented and gifted program for our entire county. This individual had no teaching experience whatsoever, yet he was asked to prepare a proposal for a countywide program. Not surprisingly, the proposal was a compilation of textbook ideas. Ned's needs, in particular, were not part of his concerns.

It was time to draw up Ned's IEP for the following year. Grasping for ideas and support, I contacted the head of the special education department at the University of Tennessee and refreshed his memory regarding Ned. He told me that I was correct in what I felt that Ned needed, and he offered me much consolation in this period of extreme frustration. I will always remember the moment he said, "You're not crazy." He said that he was available to attend our spring M-Team meeting and to speak on Ned's behalf. He gave me much ammunition to use in IEP deliberations. He also told me that I should contact another East Tennessee parent who had eventually had to go to due process on behalf of her children. I did not act on this suggestion until one year later.

Ned's IEP for the following year was agreed upon, but I continued to exert pressure on the system to hire another teacher who was trained in working with the gifted. I spoke with the superintendent on more than one occasion and voiced my concerns. Though I had been told time after time that it would be impossible for a new teacher to be hired until after the new budget would be approved in August, the teacher I had found signed a contract in early July.

Ned thus began his fourth grade year with this new special education teacher. In the late fall Ned began to have socialization problems, especially in the regular classroom. Also, numerous services promised in the IEP — both in special education and also in the regular classroom — were not provided. Ned was not challenged, and the year took a downward turn. The regular classroom teacher admitted that she was not meeting Ned's academic needs and that he needed to be in an environment where he was among children more his intellectual equal.

I began my formal request that the system consider changing placement for Ned for the following year. By this time, a new supervisor of special education was in charge. The former supervisor had been relieved of the special education portion of his position. Both of these individuals would retire within one year. Though extremely nice people, neither had the proper background to be in this position.

The LEA's reaction to my formal request started a lengthy episode which has, to date, brought us the closest yet to a due process hearing. The details are too intricate to explain fully within this framework, but the essence is the same as the problems we had earlier. The system responded with information that I did not believe, and I found it necessary to contact state officials for responsible answers and to take it upon myself to do a great deal of footwork.

A high official within the SEA program compliance administration agreed to meet with me to discuss remarks and information that the LEA had given me in response to my request. One of his reactions that particularly sticks in my mind was his response "That is the most absurd thing I have ever heard." He volunteered to take my question regarding placement to the legal department in the SEA and to inform me of the findings. This individual would be helpful to me in many ways in the several months ahead. He guided me in the writing of a request that a M-Team meeting be held, he attended one of the many M-Team meetings held at the close of the school year, and he provided valuable input that facilitated the development of an appropriate IEP.

The system made many mistakes in dealing with my request that a change in placement be considered. At our first M-Team meeting on this matter in January, the special education teacher said with great authority, "By law, we cannot consider next year until April." After this meeting it became clear that, once again, the parents would have to take the lead in taking the appropriate steps. Once again, I contacted the head of the department of special education at the University of Tennessee. I arranged for Ned to meet with him so that he could help me ascertain Ned's specific needs.

This educator was helpful, interested, and once again willing to attend an M-Team meeting to speak on behalf of the needs of the gifted, and Ned in particular. But perhaps his most helpful gesture was his reiteration that I should contact the parents to whom he had referred me one year earlier. This parent was Wendy Rankin of Sevierville, Tennessee. Her own story appears elsewhere in the book. My husband now says, "That Wendy is a real crusader!" and he is right. I contacted Wendy, and she and I embarked on a journey that has been painful, enlightening, and rewarding.

I met with Wendy and reviewed the details of my experiences in trying to get Ned's needs met. She was appalled by much of what had taken place and informed me that there had been many procedural violations. She suggested that I contact an educational consultant who had helped with her due process hearings. Coincidentally, I had contacted him on my own regarding another matter just a few weeks previously. The ball was now rolling.

After just a few minutes of meeting with this educational consultant, I was impressed by his eagerness to help us. Instead of focusing on placement, which had been my major concern, he was more interested in determining Ned's needs. His child-oriented viewpoint has helped me have a more mature approach toward planning for our gifted children.

This consultant pointed out immediately that past IEPs as written were inappropriate. He helped me draft a letter to the system which pointed out inadequacies. My letter requested an M-Team meeting; I also asked that the system prepare a technically appropriate draft IEP for presentation at the meeting. Because the system had never before produced a technically appropriate document for Ned, it stood to reason that meeting time would be saved if the system did some basic work prior to the meeting. I gave them one month to prepare this draft. I listed the types of information needed to make the document appropriate. I submitted a sample completed goal sheet as an example of what I felt was appropriate.

The educational consultant and Wendy accompanied my husband and me to our first meeting. Despite the time given to produce an appropriate document and explicit how-to instructions, once again the document the system offered fell far short. It took five meetings and over fifteen hours of deliberation for the M-Team to come up with a document that was satisfactory to our consultants and us. Our educational consultants were the only reason we were able to obtain what was lawfully correct. The system simply did not know what an appropriate IEP was. In the end, my husband and I did not get the placement for Ned we had initially desired; but we did get an excellent document.

During all the deliberation, the LEA made many mistakes. At the very first meeting, it produced a prepared typed sheet indicating where Ned would be placed and for what reasons. This action angered our educational consultants and would have been very detrimental to the system had we decided to take this case to due process. The IEP should be completed before placement is made. There were also violations of our child's right to privacy. Other mistakes, often based on the system's ignorance, were numerous. Additionally, the system often asked our consultants for advice on what was appropriate and what would be acceptable under state monitoring procedures. Our consultants' advice prevailed on many occasions. It was almost as if our consultants were providing the system in-service sessions. We had made audio recordings of the proceedings for ourselves and the system, so everything was on record.

Having obtained an appropriate document, my husband and I were relieved that "it was over." We had invested a great deal of emotional energy and money in consultants' fees to see that the following year would be one that would benefit Ned. We were encouraged by the attitudes of the principal and staff of the school where Ned would now be placed. We nevertheless felt (and still feel) that he would be better served in an environment where the range of differences in ability level were narrower, where he could be served among others more his intellectual equal, and where he would not view himself as being treated so differently. But we did have a good document. If it were followed, there was a chance that Ned would have a good year. We felt confident that the principal would do everything in his power to make the plan work.

Wendy had stood beside us all the way. Although we had paid her for her travel expenses (each trip involved approximately 150 miles), she had given freely of her time to attend and provide expertise at our M-Team meetings. As a parent who had been through the trauma of the due process procedure, she was acutely aware of the fact that gifted children are guaranteed a free and appropriate education. She began to point out that what we had just been through was not free. Though I was somewhat content to rest our case now that we had a good, solid IEP for Ned, she saw an opportunity for crusading. She encouraged me to stand up for what was "right." The system owed us some money.

I reluctantly agreed to proceed with Wendy's idea. I must admit that it was out of gratitude for what she had done for us that I initially agreed to go along with her suggestion. Not until later would I see the value of what I was doing as an avenue of personal growth for myself and view it as something that I myself really felt needed to be done.

Wendy had discussed our case with a supervisor of special education in another LEA, and they both felt strongly that parents should not have had to go to the expense to obtain for Ned what was guaranteed him by law in the first place. She and this supervisor helped me write a letter to our system requesting that the system share the expense we had incurred. Not surprisingly, the system refused to pay. We then filed an administrative complaint with the SEA. The SEA did not have the power to make a decision in this matter, but it informed us of our right to request a due process hearing.

We informed the system that if it did not make this reimbursement, we would request a hearing. The system knew that it had made many errors in the past and that these errors would be admissible evidence in a due process hearing. Our argument was that the system's past performance in IEP development and implementation was a clear indication that we had to go "outside" for help. The system also knew that it would have to bear the cost of a due process hearing and that this cost would likely outweigh the reimbursement charges we were seeking. After many meetings regarding specifics of the request, we were granted our reimbursement.

Though our story has many strained and tense portions, we are and have always been friends with the system. Though some of the teachers in the system may be naturally wary of us, we are not viewed as hostile parents. Many teachers have said to us that they understand that our goal all along has been to get for our children what they need and are guaranteed by law. It has also been helpful that our children are relatively pleasant and easy to like. Our struggles in getting the system to do what was right for Ned have made our attempts to obtain what is appropriate for his brother much easier.

I believe that our struggles have also been helpful to the growth and development of all special education in our system. This past summer the system needed to find a new supervisor of special education, because the former supervisor of special education retired at the end of the school year. Had the system filled this position in the manner done in the past, it would have promoted one of its own people to this position as sort of a resting spot until retirement eligibility.

However, the system saw the necessity to recruit an individual educated and experienced in the field of special education. It realized that special education was not an area it could play round with any longer. I am sure that our concerns were not the only factor that brought about this realization, but I am equally sure that we helped make a difference in the system's attitude toward providing special education services. We now have a fine supervisor of special education whose goal it is to make our program tops in the state.

At this writing, I am in the midst of personal growth. I have felt the power of being able to make a difference; and it is a new, exciting, and somewhat scary feeling for me. Sometimes I wonder where I will go from here. I am not yet ready to direct my energies to a specific project. Going through a due process hearing or coming close to going through a due process hearing requires recovery time. It is definitely no picnic.

Fighting for causes makes one vulnerable. During the fight it helps to know that others have had to struggle also. If parents know that others have struggled, perhaps they will be more persistent in their own struggles. It is our hope that the details of our story will help others. But the above account, detailed as it is, does not tell the entire story. Nor is the story over. The gifted program in our system is not yet what it should be.

I encourage everyone who needs to be an advocate for his child to remember three rules: (1) Never take the first "no" for an answer. (2) Find someone knowledgeable who will listen to you and help you. (3) Be firm with the system, but nice.

Good luck!

Part III

Carnegie Units and Graduation

The Saberhagen Family

Fred, the father, is a professional science fiction and fantasy writer. Joan, the mother, is a former high school mathematics teacher. She has also worked in industry as an engineering data base manager and as the president of a small computer company. Fred completed two years of college. Joan holds a B.S. in math and an M.Ed. in math education. They live in Albuquerque, New Mexico. Jill, twenty-one is a senior university student studying literature. Eric, nineteen, is a senior university student studying chemistry. Tom, eighteen, is a sophomore university student studying mathematics and philosophy. All three children were identified as gifted and participated in gifted programs throughout their educational careers.

Negotiating a Settlement with a Reticent School Administration: A Success Story

Our problem was the administration's refusal to grant our son credit for a high school geometry class which he completed while still enrolled in an elementary school. The proceedings ran from April 1986 to June 1988.

Our son, Thomas, is gifted in mathematics. Fortunately, through most of elementary school he had superior teachers who allowed him to develop this gift. In the seventh grade he was enrolled in an honors class in algebra that qualified him for a high school honors geometry class.

In the eighth grade he successfully completed honors geometry at a nearby high school, walking from his home school to high school and back again every day. Thomas was the first student in a large southwestern school district to attend elementary and high school classes during the same term.

We had been alerted at the start of the term that a certain school rule might be construed to prevent his being given high school credit for the geometry class. Nevertheless, we decided that honors geometry was the proper course for him at that stage of his mathematical education. We felt confident of this because Joan has a master's degree in math education, and many years' experience as a high school mathematics teacher.

At the end of the term, we requested that Thomas be awarded high school credit for the high school honors geometry class. Our request was denied. The school's stated reason for withholding the credit was Thomas' status as an elementary student. This classification was based solely on age, not on ability or work performed.

In our opinion, this denial was not only unfair but illegal, as it deprived our son of property he had justly earned, and which was routinely awarded to others completing the same tasks.

Potentially this refusal to give credit had serious adverse consequences. Lack of the credit might force him to complete three more years of mathematics in high school to satisfy state graduation requirements. But at the end of two years of high school he would have exhausted the standard mathematics offerings. His third required year would have had to be done in joint enrollment with the local university, where he would be required to complete Calculus III and then Differential Equations. Differential Equations is traditionally a college sophomore level class, required of only the most technically or scientifically oriented college majors. Thomas would have been *required* to take this class to earn a standard high school diploma. This, we thought, was unjust and restrictive, and certainly not the intention of the state law requiring three years' credit in high school mathematics. Our son has strong interests and talents other than mathematics, and we wanted him free to explore those fields as well.

As we considered the situation, we recognized other potential problems resulting from the denial of credit for the geometry class. Were we to move out of the local school district before Thomas completed high school, he might be required to repeat the geometry class at the new school.

On examining college entrance requirements for certain prestigious colleges, especially technically renowned schools, we found that high school geometry credit was required for entrance. Administrators at those colleges might waive the requirement, but then again they might not. The burden of proof that the district had cheated him would be on us.

In April of 1986, a few months before the end of the course, we began inquiring if Thomas would be given high school credit for the geometry class that he was obviously going to complete successfully.

On speaking with the classroom teacher, we discovered that no credit was to be given to Thomas. A school policy was being interpreted to restrict the awarding of high school credit to students in the ninth to twelfth grades only. The geometry class would appear on Thomas' record with his grade, but not with a credit.

Dissatisfied, we called the administrator in charge of special education for our area of the city. He said he was unable to help. When called, the mathematics coordinator for the city also said she was unable to offer any help. The curriculum director for the city, reached by phone, agreed to mail us a copy of the policy under which Tom was being deprived of credit, and to send a copy of our request to the superintendent of the district. The superintendent, the curriculum director said, was the only one who could initiate a reconsideration of policy.

A week later, we received a copy of the policy. It did indeed state that only high school students could receive credit for high school courses. All requirements for completing high school were to be met between the ninth and twelfth grade.

We formally requested that the superintendent reconsider the policy in light of Thomas' situation, one which growing numbers of students would face in succeeding years. A superior and progressive elementary mathematics program in the city was beginning to produce a crop of very young advanced math students. Our attempts to contact the superintendent directly had no success for a long time. She was out of town. When she returned, she did not answer our calls.

We contacted a member of our school board. She approached the curriculum committee, but was told that any change in the policy was unlikely. The policy was meant to insure that every student had a full day of high school classes and that no student would be able to finish high school early.

It was now the middle of May. The superintendent, after skillfully avoiding our phone calls for weeks, finally spoke with us briefly. She curtly informed us that she did not want to know our reasons for feeling the policy should be changed. Nor was she willing to discuss the purpose of denying credit. She saw no reason to consider a change in policy, and that was that. End of discussion.

We called the two local gifted organizations: Society for Gifted and Talented Students (SGTS) and the local Association for Gifted and Talented. We were given advice on some possible avenues by which to proceed. First, there was a special due process hearing to which children under special education were entitled when questioning administrative decisions. Second, the state education department might have jurisdiction over our situation.

Both pieces of advice were useful. First, we pursued the due process route but found that this did not apply to gifted students of special education enrolled in the specially designated mathematics classes which had allowed Thomas to do advanced work. We were not to be granted a due process hearing.

We called the State Department of Education. People there were more sympathetic but very cautious of infringing on local school board decisions. They believed a relevant memo from the state mathematics coordinator, in the form of a copy of an informal recommendation from North Central Accreditation, had been sent to the school district some time earlier. The memo requested that special cases of advanced elementary school students taking high school courses be considered for credit. Also, we learned that a program in the southern part of the state had successfully granted credits with no disastrous effects to the system, and no objections from the state.

When we again contacted our local administrators and asked about the memorandum from the state mathematics coordinator recommending credit, we were told the memo could not be located. Now their position was that any changes would have to come from the State.

Again contacting the State Department of Education, we were told definitely that any changes would have to come from the local school administration. But we could use the state superintendent's name and informally quote him as saying he saw no reason for not granting the credit. The local school administration refused to take responsibility, to reconsider its position of not granting credit, or even to give any reason for its refusal beyond the existence of a policy.

Totally frustrated, on July 14, 1986, we contacted a lawyer recommended by the local gifted societies. A few years earlier, he had won a suit against the local school board, requiring that gifted mathematics students be given instruction appropriate to their level of achievement. This allowed high school students to enroll jointly and receive credit for courses taken at the local college. A court-appointed instructor was to provide advanced elementary instruction to high-potential mathematics students. It was through the program initiated by this case situation that Thomas had received the superb instruction that enabled him to develop his talent.

An acceptable agreement was reached without actually going to court. Our lawyer negotiated with legal counsel representing the school district. He carefully and formally presented our petition in light of a civil rights violation on the basis of age discrimination. Every other student who successfully completed the honors geometry course received credit. He presented our arguments on the effect of not granting credit as limiting Thomas' options for high school enrichment. Our lawyer also showed precedent for our request from school districts within the state and the nation. And we had evidence of a case within the school district where credit had been granted by special order of a principal, contrary to the stated policy.

Several formal hearings with both lawyers, members of the administration, and ourselves were called. Records were kept, and people on both sides had the experience of being questioned as they might be in court. Our distinct impression is that had we not convinced the school district that we were ready and willing to expend the time and money necessary to undertake a federal suit, no settlement could have been reached.

In May 1986, more than two years after our first futile attempts at discussion, the superintendent and the board of education offered a settlement. Thomas was to receive high school credit for the disputed geometry class, and for a high school equivalent algebra class he had taken in seventh grade. All students who took the algebra class prior to Thomas were offered the option of receiving high school credit for that course.

A committee composed of the school district personnel, a representative from the local association for the gifted, and a parent of a gifted child was to be formed to review the gifted education program in the school district. They were to report to the board of education and the administration.

Our legal fees were partially paid by the board of education. We agreed not to pursue further litigation. Our lawyers agreed not to pursue litigation for children similarly situated to Thomas in claims against the board. Should the state decide not to recognize these credits, and to challenge Thomas' meeting the state requirements in mathematics, it was our sole responsibility to defend the authenticity of these credits. We could not require the school district to join with us in any such litigation. The board of education declined to renew the contract of the superintendent mentioned above.

We believe the refusal was in part a result of our case.

For the most part, we were pleased with the outcome. Thomas received credit for the high school courses he had taken. The school district was forced to recognize serious inequities in the system of granting credit and requiring credits for graduation.

We wish the agreement had included a statement that all future elementary students taking high school courses would be given high school credit. In May 1990, we heard that, under a new administrator, this will indeed be done. However, once Thomas was granted credit, we had no legal basis to press our claims any further. Parents of the next group of gifted children will have to carry on the fight. We hope our case will strengthen their claims.

We faced an unyielding, uncommunicative administration who felt able to disregard the concerns of individual parents. Our impression was that the superintendent and her close supporters in the school district were primarily concerned with preserving stated policies. The system's ability and willingness to deal with unique or exceptional situations was zero.

We had considered the school administrators' mandate from the people to be that of providing the best possible education to each student. But many of the administrators we dealt with gave the impression of being intent only on preserving a system they had created, regardless of the effect on a particular student.

We think that there were significant information gaps that hindered the resolution of the dispute. The following estimate is based on rumor and guesswork, but from time to time it appeared that the school district, or certain people in it, feared that if the policy of denying credit were changed for people in our particular situation, horrible financial repercussions would result. The "floodgates" (we heard that phrase several times, always at second- or third-hand) once opened, an enormous number of gifted students, not only in mathematics, would take high school courses as grade school students. And somehow this was viewed as a horrendous disruption of the system.

If the administrators really held such a belief, we can only wonder why they were not celebrating the marvelous success of a system that had produced hordes of gifted, ambitious students. But it seems all too credible that they should feel all students must be held to an exact timetable of education.

By far the most helpful group to us in this process consisted of our lawyer and his professional staff. When it became obvious that we were in for a long and difficult struggle with public school administration, we began to contact the parents of children who are slightly younger than our son and mathematically gifted. Within the next year or two these children would be in Thomas' situation, taking high school geometry while still in elementary school. One set of parents was particularly supportive. They offered moral and some financial assistance.

Several of Thomas' teachers were in strong agreement that the existing policy did not justly treat gifted students. For the moral support of these teachers, who by taking even an informal stand on our behalf were making a brave statement against their employer, we were and are most grateful.

The two groups that support gifted education in our area were encouraging. But they were unable to offer any financial assistance. Nor were they able to be too vocal in their agreement with us for fear of jeopardizing a working relationship set up with the school system only after a very difficult struggle of their own.

No group, apart from the school administration itself, hindered our case. The school district, by agreeing to a settlement, avoided the necessity of ever giving any reason for its policy. The only argument against our position that we can remember hearing came from a parent worried about the effect of an "extra" class on a child's overall grade-point average. The grade-point determines the child's ultimate standing in a graduating class. Evidently, it is more important to some parents that a child be first in the class than that they receive the appropriate mathematics credits. It would seem the whole system of calculating class standing needs to be examined for inequities.

We would fight the battle again. The advice that we would give other parents is expect to spend plenty of money and time. When you have an exceptional child, you quickly become aware that large systems are not often willing or anxious to deal with the concerns of that child. If you can expend the time and/or money necessary to bring equity to a system for your child and for the few, but important others like them, I believe it is your responsibility to do so. When necessary, get a good lawyer and dig in.

Update

Thomas was ready to start his junior year in high school by the time the dispute was over. He had completed the regular high school honor program in math. As a junior, he again worked with a specially appointed instructor to complete the calculus series. In his junior year Thomas was a National Merit Scholarship Finalist. He also entered and placed third in a national essay contest. During the summer he successfully completed a course in differential equations at the local university. He left high school after three years, without a diploma, after being accepted at Rice University, where he is now majoring in mathematics and philosophy. His success proves institutions can respond to individual needs, if their policy and administrators put a high value on the individual.

The Kozara Family

Marv and Barb Kozara are teachers and reside in Michigan. Marv is in secondary social sciences and Barb is involved in gifted education, human sexuality, and affective education of children in grades two through twelve. Both hold master's degrees and have been teaching in the district in which they live for twenty-one years. While involved in political and human service community activities, they remain diligent about continued learning.

Julianna, seventeen, and Erika, fifteen, have both been identified as gifted and talented students. As within all families, each is a unique individual with her own special talents and interests. While both are academically talented, their interests vary. Julianna focuses on the arts, and human and animal rights, while Erika's interests include Spanish, volleyball, and the social aspects of high school. Erika has benefitted in numerous ways by her sister preceding her in the system. Because of Julianna's educational needs, programs and services are now in place that, combined with Erika's personal style, make four years of high school attendance appropriate for her, if it was not for her sister. This freedom of choice was our goal in pursuing the option of accelerated graduation for Julianna.

Accelerated Graduation

Like many problems for school children, Julianna's was the result of a hard and fast, no exceptions policy; a policy printed in all capitals in our md-Michigan district's high school student handbook. This paragraph forbids upward reassignment of grade levels or graduation in less than four full years of high school attendance.

Last August, we made a request of our building principal on behalf of Julianna. As an identified gifted and talented student, she had taken advantage of numerous educational opportunities, putting her in a position to complete all course and credit requirements for a diploma in a period of three years. The principal granted our request for a deviation from the policy, and she was reclassified as a senior, being given all of the rights and privileges of her assignment. We believe his decision was influenced by the following factors:

1. Her status as an identified gifted and talented student and her apparent individual educational needs.
2. Existing district policy allowing acceleration. (Early School Entry, 1973; Gifted and Talented Policy, 1985)
3. An existing Section 47.3 Gifted and Talented Advisory Council and School Improvement Committee joint recommendation outlining options for identified high school students, including accelerated graduation.
4. A district tradition and practice of educational progressiveness, based on sound research and demonstrated effectiveness.

Another issue that may have been an advantage or a complicating factor is that both of us are teachers in the system. I am the district's coordinator of services for the gifted and talented and chair of the Gifted and Talented Advisory Board. My husband is a high school teacher in the building where both of our daughters attend.

What none of us anticipated was the reaction of some board members to the recommendations of the two bodies regarding the upward extension of the current practice of acceleration, which is based on a determination of appropriateness by the administrator, staff, and parents. After lengthy discussion, only two objections surfaced. Students should not miss any of the activities of their senior year, and students would not be socially and emotionally mature if allowed early graduation. This last concern was not raised with regard to the younger children or for those who enter high school already having been accelerated. The recommendations were tabled, with the president requesting further information from the advisory at the December meeting.

Prior to that meeting, all board members were provided with copies of documents representing the current research and findings of several professionals in the field. Subsequently, a comprehensive presentation was made by five advisory council members. In this context, the considerations behind the recommendation for acceleration were discussed in detail. While no board member was aware of our child's situation or previous administrative action, it seemed best to avoid a possible political problem. I did not make the report, but I was present.

The recommendations were again tabled. It had become obvious that two things were clouding the issue in the minds of some board members. These were personal biases related to reminiscence about their own high school experience and issues regarding their own child's high school career. These things were exerting more influence than both the fact and information being presented by the people who had spent a full year developing the recommendations.

At this point, my husband and I felt it was appropriate to seek legal counsel. We perceived a distinct threat to Julianna's receiving the diploma she was working very hard to earn by June 1990. The attorney we selected was one with a reputation for having the courage to take on systems which were engaging in discrimination and violating the civil rights of individuals. We discussed all of the possibilities if the board should choose to be capricious and arbitrary in over-turning administrative action. Issues that could be pursued included age discrimination and losses related to scholar-ships only available to the valedictorian and salutatorian of the graduating class. We also discussed the difficulty in con-vincing a judge to take the political risk of granting an injunc-tion against a school board.

Administratively we were continuously reassured that in the absence of board policy dealing with gifted and talented high school students, the administrative decision to graduate our daughter would be carried out as planned. There was not much comfort in those assurances, given that we were now being made painfully aware of the feeling of some board members, including the fact that this had become a very personal issue for some of them. They are, in fact, the body which must approve all of the names on the list of graduates.

Six months after the initial presentation, the board quietly voted four to three to accept recommendations for program-ming options for high school gifted and talented students, including accelerated graduation. We were pleased with this outcome because it assures Julianna a smooth transition into university life. By June, she will have completed seventeen university credits in the social sciences while attending high school four hours a day. She will also have maintained a grade point average which places her in the position of salutatorian of the class and will be announced as the re-cipient of a four year full tuition, fees, and books scholarship from the university of her choice.

The greatest difficulty for us has been the emotional roller coaster that a situation such as this creates. It is never easy for parents to have someone else in a position to make important life decisions on behalf of their child. We would be given information that would make us feel that we could relax and then another statement or action would occur, again making us feel that our child's welfare was being threatened. This probably was worse for us than for some parents because of our employment relationship with the district.

We are respected educators with a strong history of support for, and positive contribution to, the system. As such, we felt it necessary to be very candid with the principal and superintendent about our intention to advocate for our child through any avenue available to us. We made it clear to them that we wished to avoid the adversarial role, but we considered our first obligation to be to our child. They were very respectful of our position and not surprised, since we have a long term reputation for advocating for other people's children.

Beyond the assistance of our attorney, we are most grateful to the editors of this book. They provided us with insight, encouragement, and support as we worked through this process. It helps a great deal to know there is a network of caring people who share your concern for your child's reaching her highest potential.

This battle, while more emotional than one of actual confrontation, was well worth the energy. Not only does our child have an opportunity to move ahead with fulfilling her life goals, but those who follow her have a better chance of having their individual educational needs met by the system, without having to apologize for being different.

Our advice to other parents would be to make sure they have thoroughly researched their issue and then ask the school for what their child needs. When requests are made through the proper chain of authority and are supported by facts, there is the greatest chance of avoiding conflict. If it becomes necessary to enter an adversarial role, you will be in a position to respond factually, without a great deal of emotion. There are many resource people and organizations which concern themselves with the needs of the gifted population; some are listed in the Appendices of this book. You can count on people like these to assist you in making contact with the support network. Not only can they help you gather support data, these people can provide support with the emotional aspects of your struggle.

The Markovic Family

Mr. Markovic, born in Yugoslavia, attended the University of Belgrade. He graduated with a major in electrical engineering and is presently an engineering manager. Ivana's mother, also born in Yugoslavia, graduated from college with a degree in electrical engineering technology. She is presently employed in marketing quotations for an engineering firm. The Markovics live in Lilburn, Georgia.

Ivana was born on August 2, 1972 in Belgrade, Yugoslavia. She is currently enrolled at MIT (class of 1993), has adapted to college life very well, and enjoyed being the youngest freshman there. She works hard, has taken a full load of courses, has successfully completed the freshman year and is looking forward to her sophomore year in September 1990. At MIT, her fields of interests have broadened and she has not decided on her major. She is still considering graduate study in the medical field.

Her sister, Ana, is fifteen and was born August 31, 1974, in Ottawa, Canada. She has completed her sophomore year at Parkview High, the school Ivana attended, and is ranked #1 in the class of about 430 students. Ana will spend her summer in Governor's Honors Program with a major in math. Ana is very active in many fields at school and in extracurricular activities. She has won several state level competitions in music composition, and plays violin in Atlanta Emory Orchestra and in the Atlanta Symphony Youth Orchestra. Like her sister, Ana has taken the same advanced math courses in the middle school, and could fulfill graduation requirements in her junior year; but at the moment we don't know if Ana will follow Ivana's footsteps. Based on Ivana's experiences, we wonder if it is worth it.

The Case of the Honorary High School Diploma

My daughter was a straight A student for her entire school career. She had even taken two high school math courses while still in middle school. At the end of her high school junior year, she managed to collect twenty-one Carnegie units, the requirement for obtaining a high school diploma. At that time, several top universities in the country had acknowledged those credits as valid, and she was accepted as a regular student by Georgia Tech, Emory, Vanderbilt, Duke, and Massachusetts Institute of Technology.

However, the State Board of Education did not allow two of her math credits to count for graduation because she was not in high school when she earned them. She was, therefore, denied her high school diploma.

We both feel that education is one of the most important experiences in life, and that the actual achievements are the facts that should count. As parents, we have tried to transfer our attitude toward education and achievement to our children. We also thought that the purpose of going through high school was to get a basic and general education, as well as to prepare students for specific areas of study in college.

Our children have attended gifted classes and advanced classes and have done very well in them. They have always been in the classes with the more senior students and performed up to expectations.

Students take Advanced Placement (AP) classes for particular reasons: to improve their knowledge, to fill their time with challenging work, to get ahead of the crowd, to show what they can do and at the same time to benefit themselves in several other ways, one of which is to improve their grade point averages (GPAs) or to shorten the time they must attend school. Many make sacrifices which should be appreciated and awarded. The best way to show the appreciation and to award someone is to legallay recognize their achievements by making such achievements count. It is not "child's play" to be in the eighth grade and to take on a tenth grade high school course and make an A in it. That accomplishment should be rewarded, not penalized.

In almost all cases, students' GPAs were lowered because their scores in advanced courses were below their scores in regular courses. In my daughter's case, this was not a significant problem because she made a 95 in one of these courses when her total GPA was 98.625. I do know several students who were discouraged from taking AP courses because of the big impact on their GPAs.

Last school year, we found out that striving for the best and being among the best may not always be considered positive, and may even be handicapping. High school students in this state can earn six Carnegie units per year (one per year, per each one-year course). On a regular basis, this usually totals twenty-four units. The requirement for graduation is twenty-one Carnegie units, thirteen of which may be from the list of prescribed categories for non-college bound students or seventeen from the categories prescribed for college bound students. Accordingly, an observer would think that a student who works hard and makes good grades can graduate from high school as soon as he or she earns twenty-one valid Carnegie units, thirteen or seventeen from the prescribed list. In this state, according to the current board of education policy, this is only permitted if a student is a dropout with a number of Carnegie units missing and he or she can attend summer or night school and can manage to earn enough D's or maybe C's to collect twenty-one units. This type of student will definitely receive a high school diploma and a big "atta-boy."

However, if a student is very bright, can handle work beyond a regular curriculum, attends regular public school, follows legal policies, guidelines, and rules legislated by the State Board of Education, and manages to earn twenty-one straight A's before attending the twelfth grade, he or she cannot get a high school diploma in Georgia, even though all courses would have earned full Carnegie units if taken at some other time or some other age. We experienced this latter situation in a very dramatic way during the 1988–89 school year.

In addition to regular high school courses, my daughter had taken one English course during the summer. Even when she was still attending middle school, she took two intimidating high school math courses: Algebra I and Geometry. The geometry course was taken at a nearby high school in an actual high school classroom with students from the ninth, tenth, and eleventh grades. The English course and the two math courses were from the compulsory list of courses required for high school graduation.

These courses gave her additional Carnegie units which appeared on her high school transcript as accomplished credits. Also, they counted for a college preparatory seal and were included when her average score and GPA were figured.

In November of 1988, my daughter, a junior in high school, was filling out her planning sheet for the rest of the year and for the following year. She discovered that she did not have a choice of challenging senior year courses since she had already taken several AP courses, including Calculus BC. The computer record showed that she had already earned fifteen valid Carnegie units and that six more were required for graduation. At that point, she was on her way to earning the six more units by the end of her junior year.

Ivana and her counselor concluded that she could graduate a year early, and my daughter decided to go for it. She was moved to a senior class and began checking out informative college books. Most of her teachers were very happy for her

and encouraged her in her decision. We, her parents, did not
say much, but we did not discourage her. We subsequently
helped her with the college applications.

Two weeks later, the counselor told my daughter that they
were mistaken and that the State Board of Education policy
states that her two math courses would not be counted for
graduation since they were taken while she was still in middle school! The same two courses counted for the College
Preparatory Seal, and counted in her GPA. The same two
courses would have counted for graduation if they were taken
after the completion of middle school. Since the actual requirement is that the students must take two years of any
math, many students graduated in the same school taking
only Algebra I spread over two years! My daughter took a
total of five years of math. At the time, I was convinced that
the high school diploma was the most important thing to
attach to the college application. I thought it was an absolute
"must have."

The next day, I contacted the director of the Department
of Education, Division of General Instruction. That contact
started the events which were described in the monthly *Atlanta Magazine* as "The Worst Example of Bureaucratic
Mind at Work." The Director confirmed the Board of Education's policy and gave his full endorsement of the policy. He
maintained that it is in the best interest of my daughter to
stay in high school one more year. I insisted that we and she
thought otherwise and that she had more than fulfilled the
board's requirements based on the courses she took. I
explained that this was a very discouraging, discriminating,
damaging, and unfair policy. However, he was firm, stating
that it was the law, and she should plan on returning to high
school the next school year.

I understood. Laws and policies are created by the people
and can be improved, changed, or abolished by the people.

I asked about the procedures involved in changing the policy. He suggested that I appeal the policy, and indicated that if it were changed my daughter would be allowed to graduate early.

He advised me about the regular legal route. The first step was to appeal the case to the school principal, and with his support, take the case to the County Board of Education. With the county board of education's recommendations, I could appeal to the state board where they would make a decision. He made it sound like it was a daily routine procedure, and it would take a couple of days to resolve. But he did add that he would not recommend to the board to change the policy. I did not know at the time that his statement was very crucial to the case.

The next day I was in the principal's office. He stated that he fully endorsed the policy and refused to support me, but he said that I had his approval to address the county board of education. The same day I talked to the assistant superintendent of the county schools. He was very supportive and sympathetic of my daughter's case, gave me some good advice, and asked me to write to him so he could present the case to the Board of Education in time for their session on December 22.

I attended the meeting. My case was not scheduled on the agenda, but I did get the chance to address the board in person. The county superintendent explained that this was the state's policy and the counties could not change it nor could they act against it (like grant a waiver from the policy to my daughter). He said that I was getting a raw deal in the way I was directed to pursue my case and that I was misinformed as far as who had authority to change the policy or to grant a waiver from it. He advised me to address the state's board of education immediately, and he recommended to the county's board of education to write me a letter backing me up and giving me full support.

The letter arrived in mid-January. I rewrote my appeal, sent it to the state board of education, and waited for the call or letter. I was hoping that I would be able to address the state board in January and possibly resolve the case in time to beat the deadline for the college scholarship applications.

I changed the wording on my appeal to make it unmistakably clear that I was asking for the policy to be changed first. In plain English, I requested the following two things:

1. For the state board of education to change the policy.
2. In case the board decided to change the policy, and if the process about policy change took too much time to complete beyond June, then I asked for my daughter to be allowed to graduate in June.

Several days after the January board session, I received a call from the Department of Education's legal assistant. He reports to the director of the Department of Education, and one of his duties is to make sure that the cases which reach the board of education are in the proper legal format. From then on he was the only contact I had with the Department of Education. He was merely doing his job and executing the orders of the director.

After a decision had been made, he broke the news to me: The case did not reach the board. He was preparing the cases for the February session and he wanted to know exactly what I wanted. Was my main objective to appeal the policy or for my daughter to get a high school diploma? I explained that I wanted my daughter to get a high school diploma which she has earned, but I knew this could happen only if the policy was changed. Therefore, I first wanted the policy changed and then the new policy be applied to my daughter's case.

He said that he would send some papers for me to sign. Also, he asked if I would like to address the Special Instructional Committee (part of the board) for their information only, on the condition that there would be no ruling upon the case. I promptly accepted his suggestion.

Before I got the chance to appear in front of the committee, my daughter received her first acceptance letter from Atlanta's Emory University. That gave us all tremendous relief and made the further appeals unnecessary. Nevertheless, I was convinced that the policy was not doing a good service to education since it did not encourage students to strive for excellence. I thought that perhaps the policy's impact was not known to the board and that all it would take was someone to come forward and point out the facts. I wrote a good explanation of the workings of the policy, pointing out the benefits of its change.

I came to the meeting and tried to read my memo to make sure that all of the facts would be presented. Halfway through, I was interrupted by a committee member who rather rudely asked such questions as "Who do you think you are by asking for your daughter to graduate before she is supposed to?" I was given a lecture indicating that I could not just come in on their meeting and ask for decisions.

I angrily responded that I was commissioned to come and was only there to talk for their benefit, that no giveaways were needed from them, and that what was thought to be a problem was resolved in that my daughter had already received one college acceptance letter and therefore was sure to be in college next year! I never finished my speech.

A short discussion followed. I learned that other "unreasonable parents" had tried to push their children through graduation too soon when they shouldn't have. There were other ways to get a high school diploma, such as early admission, joint enrollment, night school, taking the GED test, and summer school. If my daughter hurried, she could still take and finish two elective courses at night school and qualify for graduation in June. Any two elective courses would count! Any two but algebra and geometry. Deep down, I thought (and I still do) that these two math courses were many times more valuable than any elective course taken at night school.

Even though I really did not need to anymore, I decided to continue for the benefit of other students who may get in the same position. I called the Legal Office of the Department of Education the next day and told them that I still wanted to pursue the policy change.

I talked to the legal office daily, and they assured me that the case would reach the board. Two days before the board meeting in February, I received the whole package in the mail. It was returned to me because I was missing the actual "decision" from the county board of education and the proof that the case was on the board's agenda!

I wrote another letter to the county board and took it inperson to the county superintendent. He was disappointed. The state's policies were not in the jurisdiction of the county board! Another month was lost because the county's meeting followed the state's meeting. (County and state boards meet once a month and the state precedes the county by several days.)

The county superintendent added my case to the agenda of the county board meeting, which I attended. The ruling was very brief, and it was concluded that they were not in jurisdiction to change such a policy nor could they act against it. They agreed that the policy should change and that they would write a letter in support of my case. They said that they regretted that this policy matter was not in their jurisdiction as they would gladly change it.

Several days later I received a letter and forwarded the whole case again to the state board, now with proof in black and white that the case was "treated" at the county level. In the phone conversation that followed with the board's legal assistant, I was told that they had everything in the required format and that the case would not miss the March session. Along the way, we were talking about my options in case the board did not rule in my favor. The legal assistant advised me that I could appeal the case immediately to the Supreme Court of Georgia and that there were still chances that the court could overturn the board's decision before the end of the school year. He referred to a number of cases which ended up like that.

One day before the March meeting of the state board, I received a letter from the legal assistant in which I was told that the appeal as such must be written by the county superintendent, and that his signature on the appeal was required before the state board could "treat it." The next day I took the letter to the county superintendent, apologizing for all the inconvenience that I caused him and his office, and offered to drop the case if he told me to do so. He could not hide his anger, and when he reached the legal assistant on the phone he literally yelled. The legal assistant checked all the papers in my file and admitted that he actually had everything he needed. One more month was lost. The next session would be in April, and then they would take a break in May. I was waiting to see what would be invented to create the next roadblock.

Meanwile, my daughter was accepted by Georgia Tech, Vanderbilt, Duke, and MIT. Now, instead of worrying whether she would go to college next year, our worry became which college she would attend.

While waiting for the April session, a local news reporter who had attended the county's board meeting in December of 1988, called to see how my case was resolved. When I told him the status, he wrote a story about it. Several TV reports followed his story. One involved an interview with the director of the Department of Education. In the interview, he explained what the advanced classes were all about. According to the director, the AP classes were developed so that students could advance in their education, not by finishing school faster, but for them to have a good high school career! (Excuse me, but what is a good high school career, please? I thought that the prime goal for high school should be to prepare students for college!)

Reaction from the media and the press probably forced the issue. People were writing letters. Because of the public response, there were no more roadblocks. I knew that this time the case would be treated. I was eagerly preparing for the meeting and I knew that I could argue different aspects against the policy for hours and hours.

But soon, with one week's notice, I was told that the case would definitely be on the agenda in the morning Board session on April 14, 1989, if I agreed that they do it in a closed session without me being able to address the board. The actual reasons were never clearly explained to me, but several explanations were offered. One was that there was not enough time to prepare for the case. I was told that in the case of a negative ruling, I would be instructed to appeal the case immediately to the Supreme Court, and that the chances were very good that it would go very well. If I disagreed, then the case appearance would have to be moved to the end of May or sometime in the summer. I had no choice but to accept.

The final day, April 14, 1989, came. I was at work when the big disappointment was handed out to me over the phone. The press and TV reporters were waiting there for the ruling. One of the TV reporters called me to find out my reaction and my next plans. I said I was very disappointed and that I had to forfeit my appearance in front of the Board, otherwise such a sad outcome may not have happened. I also said to everyone that I may proceed through the court, but that we were not badly hurt since the top universities in the country did not think that a high school diploma from Georgia was worth much anyway. My daughter would be going to MIT regardless of the ruling.

I called the legal assistant and he confirmed the negative outcome. He promised to put the official papers in the mail promptly so that time wouldn't be wasted for appealing the case. The forms for appealing would also be included, and all I had to do was sign and return them.

The news about the board's ruling spread rapidly through the press, TV, and radio. Several local radio stations did a talk show on April 14, all day and for a few hours late at night. The story of the local news reporter who had attended the December 1988 county board meeting was picked up by the Associated Press. Two nationally syndicated radio stations transmitted the story and the interview with my daughter and myself.

Then the official letter from the board came. It was a big joke, but not a funny one. I wish I had known its contents when I was interviewed by reporters and when I was on the talk show. The case was distorted and mishandled. The State Board of Education, the supreme body for education in the state, did not understand (or elected not to understand) plain English sentences I wrote down in my appeal.

The case was treated as *Mr. Milan Markovic vs. Gwinnet County Board of Education*. The ruling was done as if I was appealing the decision of the county board of education not to grant a waiver of the state's policy to my daughter. Even at my first appeal to the Gwinnet County Board I asked for the policy to be changed first and then — only if it became necessary — to consider a waiver of the policy. The state board knew that no other ruling could have been possible at the county level.

Now I understand why the director of the Department of Education insisted that the case must be treated at the county level before it could reach the state level. Then the case could be presented upside down to the board of education. Also, I understood the reasons for the need for the special, private session without me being given a chance to address the board. I was sure that some board members had not read my appeal in whole, because they could not possibly have missed a number of the arguments that I had in the appeal. Of the two positive votes, one was by the committee member who interrupted my speech during February's session and to whom I addressed my angry remarks. He probably gave my comments some thought afterwards. I am sure I would have gotten three more votes if the board members could have heard me. In the official ruling, however, the request for the policy change was never mentioned.

I do consider myself an intelligent person. I knew that my daughter did not meet the policy, and I never requested that she get her high school diploma regardless of the policy. I appealed the policy and requested the policy change, and I did it in the way the director of the Department of Education instructed me to do it. I followed his instructions every step of the way!

When I called the legal assistant and complained that this was not my case, he explained to me how that was the only way that the board could have looked into it. He explained that the policies are not created or changed upon the suggestions of the citizens or upon appeals similar to mine. It is a long legislative process that is triggered internally in board sessions or by another body of the Department of Education, and the result of the process is never predictable. Definitely, it is not something that the board would resolve in one session, especially when based on the appeal of some individual who does not like it.

I then understood why Georgia holds a solid forty-eighth place in education and why it will stay there for a long time. I wonder why it is not fiftieth. If the Department of Education is playing such games, and if the State Board of Education could not understand my appeal, then we have a real sad situation here. I can guarantee that any sixth grader would understand from my letters that the change of policy was the primary purpose of my appeal.

I concluded that further efforts would be meaningless. At this rate, it would take a lifetime. It was for a good cause, but I was fighting with people who were not using logic and common sense. Their minds were set and nothing in the world would make them think or listen. After seven months of debating on the issues, highly positioned people with Ph.D. titles behind their names were showing me that they did not understand plain English.

The official letter contained one more "joke"; this was the notice of the right to appeal. But the automatic appeal was not to the Supreme Court as I was told. It was addressed to the Superior Court of Gwinnett County, and the plaintiff was the Gwinnett County Board of Education! And for all this time, the Gwinnett County Board of Education was my partner in the case, supporting me and cosigning my appeal with me. Now, I was supposed to take the County Board of Education to County Superior Court because they followed the law and "ruled negative" back in February. I did not find much sanity in this reasoning.

The Gwinnett County Board of Education, in their next session, decided to grant an Honorary High School Diploma to my daughter as their token of appreciation for her achievements since they could not grant her a regular diploma. She was invited to take part in the graduation ceremony, and she was there, proudly walking in line with the honor graduates. It was a very, very nice gesture by the Gwinnett County Board of Education.

Still, in one way we have come out shortchanged. In school, my daughter was treated as a junior until the very end; therefore, she could not compete for any of the scholarships regularly available to seniors. Many students, some way behind her on the rating list, have received full scholarships. She did not get a single cent, even though she was one of the top three students in both the junior and senior classes combined!

My daughter proceeded with her plans and enrolled at MIT. She has adapted excellently to college life, and she is handling college assignments very well. With my wife and her sister, I must finish by saying that we are very proud of her.

Final Remarks

I would like to add a few comments to the above. Time was a big factor in this case. This was a fact known to the officials from the Department of Education. They have all the time in the world to drag the cases for years. Parents and students usually have only a few months to resolve conflict. After a few months, most parents have no interest in continuing a losing battle. Now I have to worry about helping my daughter through college, and this case for us is history. Government officials count on this. Whether my daughter's case has a happy ending is hard to tell. I think that we have lost anyway. The policy did not change nor will it change in the near future.

It is a sad fact that the system is designed to suppress, in many different ways, the pursuit for excellence in education of these diligent, ambitious, and capable children.

In addition to the long bureaucratic battle with the system, these children often have a hard time at school, being mistreated by their peers. Not being supported by the legal education system, they are at a disadvantage. They are often not warmly accepted.

Parents of students who plan to shorten the time it takes to get to college should take all this into consideration, as well as the following on the financial side of education. The system definitely does not make it worthwhile to accelerate their education. These students are not counted as seniors and their names are not included in the running for any of the grants and scholarships available to seniors.

As I mentioned earlier, the seniors last year at my daughter's school received approximately 1.7 million dollars in grants and scholarship funds. Over 300 different scholarships ranking from partial ones with as little as $300, to full scholarships with tuition, board, etc. were awarded. My daughter, being entangled in the bureaucratic battle and not being counted as a senior, could not compete for a single dollar.

Finally, the last punch. Recently, I have met some parents of talented middle school students who, like my daughter, are capable of handling above average class loads. They were looking forward to taking advanced courses in math and they inquired about these courses at the beginning of the year. But, they will definitely not get into the situation to challenge board of education policies about eligibility for graduation. Georgia Board of Education has found a way not to get into embarrassment again. Students are not allowed to take advanced courses! The reason explained to their parents: If they do take advanced courses in middle school, they will not have anything to take later when they are in high school!

Given the vast amount of exciting and challenging material available for study in the world today, I hope the Georgia Board of Education changes the policy and allows gifted students to complete the advanced courses when the students are ready to devour them. This change would then allow those students to progress to other areas of study and maintain a high level of intellectual stimulation.

Afterword

The parents who fought these battles for their gifted children deserve our praise and congratulations. Not only have these parents improved the lives of their own children, but in many cases they have succeeded in paving the way for other students to achieve intellectual goals. And although all the parents agreed the struggle was worth it, at times the sacrifices have been high in both economic and emotional costs.

The reader may be left with the question of why in America these struggles have to occur in the first place. Are we suspicious of intellectuals while readily endorsing less cognitive activities? Has the leveling process in American democracy invaded the educational sphere to the extent that we have become desensitized to the needs of the intellectually gifted? Or, is it that policymakers are unaware of the rewards for society in serving the needs of the intellectually advantaged?

Thankfully, for the health of the nation, the answer is hopefully none of the above. Instead, we live in a world of limited resources where a bevy of programs must compete in Congress with appropriations for defense, medical research, social programs, and maintenance of the nation's infrastructure. In the state legislatures, funding for highways, economic development, and general educational expenses often preclude adequate financial support for the gifted. And at both level of government, gifted education advocates are often competing against entrenched and well-financed lobbies who are professionals at operating in the political arena.

Therefore, for gifted education to prosper in our democratic system, it is going to be necessary for advocates, just as those interested in children with other special needs have championed their cause, to continue to educate legislators, school personnel, parents, and the general public of the essentiality of providing greater resources for America's gifted children. Several of the appendices in this book provide resources to start such an educational process.

The successes, recounted in this compendium of stories by parents, suggest that if gifted education advocates at every level continue to strive for the nation's resources to appropriately assist outstanding students, perhaps in the not too distant future, we will have a federal law mandating appropriate education for America's gifted youth. The efforts described by the parents in these stories truly provide inspiration and hope for all of us.

Suggested Readings

Berger, S. L. (1990). *Supporting gifted education through advocacy.* Reston, VA: The Council for Exceptional Children.

Ginsberg-Riggs, G. (1984). Parent power: Wanted for organization. *Gifted Child Quarterly, 28*(3), pp. 111–14.

Hall, E. G. & Skinner, N. (1980). *Somewhere to turn: Strategies for parents of the gifted and talented.* New York: Teachers College Press.

Gallagher, J. J. (1983). A model for advocacy for gifted education. In J. Gallagher, S. Kakpan, & I. Sato (eds.) *Promoting the education of the gifted/talented: Strategies for advocacy* (pp. 1–9). Ventura, CA: The National/State Leadership Training Institute on the Gifted and Talented.

Karnes, F. A. & Marquardt, R. (1991). *Gifted children and the law: mediation, due process, and court cases.* Dayton, OH: Ohio Psychology Press.

Kraver, T. (1981). Parent power: Starting and building a parent organization. In P. B. Mitchell (ed.), *An advocate's guide to building support for gifted and talented education* (pp. 24–30). Washington, DC: National Association of State Boards of Education.

Mitchell, P. B. (1981). Effective advocacy: Understanding the process and avoiding the pitfalls. In P. B. Mitchell (ed.), *An advocate's guide to building support for gifted and talented education* (pp. 5–23). Washington, DC: National Association of State Boards of Education.

Tannenbaum, A. J. (1980). *Reaching out: Advocacy for the gifted and talented.* New York: Teachers College Press.

Tuttle, F. B., Jr. (1980). *Gifted and talented children: How parents can help.* Washington, DC: National Education Association.

Appendix A

State Consultants
in Gifted Education

Alabama

Program for Exceptional Children
Alabama State Department of Education
1020 Monticello Court
Montgomery, AL 36117

Alaska

Gifted and Talented Education
Department of Special Services
P.O. Box F
Juneau, AK 99811-9981

American Samoa

Gifted/Talented Education
American Samoa Department of Education
Pago Pago, AS 96799

Arizona

Arizona Department of Education
1535 West Jefferson
Phoenix, AZ 85007

Arkansas

Programs for Gifted/Talented
Room 105-C, Education Building
4 Capitol Mall
Little Rock, AR 72201

California

Gifted and Talented Education
California Department of Education
P.O. Box 944272
Sacramento, CA 94244-2720

Colorado

Gifted and Talented Education
Colorado Department of Education
201 East Colfax
Denver, CO 80203

Connecticut

Gifted/Talented Programs
Connecticut Department of Education
25 Industrial Park Road
Middletown, CT 06457

Delaware

Gifted and Talented Programs
Delaware Department of Instruction
P.O. Box 1402
Townsend Building
Dover, DE 19903

District of Columbia

Gifted/Talented Education Program
Nalle School
50th and C Street SE
Washington, DC 20029

Florida

Gifted Program
Bureau of Exceptional Children
Florida Department of Education
654 Florida Education Centre
Tallahassee, FL 32399-0400

Georgia

Gifted Education
Division of General Instruction
Georgia Department of Education
1952 Twin Towers East
Atlanta, GA 30334-5040

Guam

GATE
Department of Education
P.O. Box DE
Agana, GU 96910

Hawaii

Gifted and Talented
Office of Instructional Services
189 Lunalilo Home Road
Honolulu, HI 96825

Idaho

Idaho Department of Education
Len B. Jordan Office Building
650 West State
Boise, ID 83720

Illinois

Curriculum Improvement Section N-242
Illinois Board of Education
100 North First Street
Springfield, IL 62777

Indiana

Gifted and Talented
Indiana Department of Education
229 State House
Indianapolis, IN 46204

Iowa

Gifted Education
Department of Education
Grimes State Office Building
Des Moines, IA 50319-0146

Kansas

Gifted/Talented Education
Kansas Department of Education
120 East 10th
Topeka, KS 66612

Kentucky

Gifted/Talented Education
Kentucky Department of Education
1831 Capitol Plaza Tower
Frankfort, KY 40601

Louisiana

Gifted/Talented Program
Louisiana Department of Education
P.O. Box 94064
Baton Rouge, LA 70804-9064

Maine

Gifted/Talented Programs
Maine Department of Education
    and Cultural Services
State House Station #23
Augusta, ME 04333

Maryland

Gifted/Talented Division
Maryland Department of Education
200 W. Baltimore Street
Baltimore, MD 21201

Massachusetts

Gifted/Talented
Bureau of Curriculum Service
Massachusetts Department of Education
1385 Hancock Street
Quincy, MA 02169

Michigan

Gifted and Talented
Michigan Department of Education
P.O. Box 30008
Lansing, MI 48909

Minnesota

Gifted Education
Minnesota Department of Education
550 Cedar Street
St. Paul, MN 55101

Mississippi

Gifted and Talented
Bureau of Special Service
Mississippi Department of Education
P.O. Box 771
Jackson, MS 39205-0771

Missouri

Gifted Education
Missouri Department of Elementary
    and Secondary Education
P.O. Box 480
100 East Capitol
Jefferson City, MO 65102

Montana

Gifted/Talented
Office of Public Instruction
State Capitol
Helena, MT 59620

Nebraska

Gifted/Talented Program
Nebraska Department of Education
P.O. Box 94987
300 Centennial Mall South
Lincoln, NE 68509

Nevada

Gifted/Talented Program
Special Education Branch
Nevada Department of Education
400 West King Street
Capitol Complex
Carson City, NV 89710

New Hampshire

Gifted Education
New Hampshire Department
   of Education
101 Pleasant Street
Concord, NH 03301

New Jersey

Gifted and Talented
Division of General Academic Education
New Jersey Department of Education
225 W. State Street, CN 500
Trenton, NJ 08625-0500

New Mexico

Gifted/Talented Special Education
Education Building
Santa Fe, NM 87501-2786

New York

Gifted Education
New York Department
   of Education
Room 212 EB
Albany, NY 12234

North Carolina

Gifted Education
Division for Exceptional Children
North Carolina Department
  of Public Instruction
116 W. Edenton St., Education Bldg.
Raleigh, NC 27603-1712

North Dakota

Gifted and Talented Education
North Dakota Department
  of Public Instruction
State Capitol
Bismarck, ND 58505

Ohio

Gifted Education
Ohio Division of Special Education
933 High Street
Worthington, OH 43085

Oklahoma

Gifted and Talented Section
Oklahoma Department of Education
2500 N. Lincoln Blvd.
Oklahoma City, OK 73105

Oregon

Gifted and Talented Specialist
700 Pringle Parkway SE
Salem, OR 97219

Pennsylvania

Gifted and Talented
Bureau of Special Education
Pennsylvania Department of Education
333 Market Street
Harrisburg, PA 17126-0333

Puerto Rico

Gifted Education
Puerto Rico Department of Education
Office of External Resources
Hato Rey, PR 99024

Rhode Island

Gifted and Talented Education
Department of Elementary and
   Secondary Education
22 Hayes Street
Providence, RI 02908

South Carolina

Gifted Program
802 Rutledge Building
1429 Senate Street
Columbia, SC 29201

South Dakota

Gifted Programs
Special Education Section
North Dakota Department of Education
700 North Illinois
Richard F. Kneip Building
Pierre, SD 57501

Tennessee

Gifted and Talented Programs and Services
Tennessee Department of Education
132-A Cordell Hull Building
Nashville, TN 37219

Texas

Gifted and Talented
Texas Education Agency
1701 N. Congress Avenue
Austin, TX 78701

Trust Territory

Federal Programs Coordinator
Office of Special Education
Trust Territory Office of Education
Office of the High Commissioner
Saipan, CM 96950

Utah

Gifted and Talented Education
Utah Department of Education
250 E. 500 South
Salt Lake City, UT 84111

Vermont

Gifted Education
Vermont Department of Education
Montpelier, VT 05602

Virgin Islands

Gifted/Talented Education
St. Thomas/St. John School District
#44-46 Kongens Gade
St. Thomas, VI 00802

Virginia

Gifted Programs
Virginia Department of Education
P.O. Box 6-Q
Richmond, VA 23216-2060

Washington

Gifted Programs
Superintendent of Public Instruction
Old Capitol Building FG-11
Olympia, WA 98504

West Virginia

Gifted Programs
Office of Special Education
West Virginia Department of Education
Capitol Building 6, Room B-304
Charleston, WV 25305

Wisconsin

Gifted and Talented Program
Wisconsin Department of Public Instruction
P.O. Box 7841
125 S. Webster
Madison, WI 53707

Wyoming

Language Arts, Gifted and Talented
Wyoming Department of Education
Hathaway Building
Cheyenne, WY 82002

• • •

Appendix B

National and International Professional Associations and Advocacy Groups for Gifted Children and Adults

American Association for Gifted Children
Talent Identification Program
Duke University
Box 40077
Durham, NC 27706-0077

This association has research as its primary focus. The AAGC strives to assist similar organizations in gifted education.

American Mensa, Ltd.
2626 East 14th Street
Brooklyn, NY 11235-3992

Mensa is an organization for highly intelligent persons with membership determined on a standardized intelligence test score higher than 98 percent of the general population. The organization sponsors meetings and publications.

The Association for the Gifted (TAG)
Council for Exceptional Children
1920 Association Drive
Reston, VA 22091

TAG is a division of the Council for Exceptional Children. Publications include books, a journal, and a newsletter. They are involved in legislative activity on behalf of gifted children.

The Council of State Directors of Programs for Gifted
G/T Programs Consultant
Maine Department of Education
and Cultural Services
State House Station #23
Augusta, ME 04333

The Council is composed of state directors of gifted and talented programs. Their primary focus is the development and dissemination of current information on gifted education across the United States.

Gifted Child Society, Inc.
190 Rock Road
Glen Rock, NJ 07452

The society was founded to further the cause of gifted education through educational and support services. Special programs and services are also available for parents and other adults.

The Institute for Law and Gifted Education
909 South 34th Avenue
Hattiesburg, MS 39402

The Institute serves as a clearinghouse for legal issues involving gifted students. It offers workshops, seminars, and consultations.

The National Association for Creative Children and Adults
8080 Springvalley Drive
Cincinnati, OH 45236

This group focuses on the development and nurturing of creativity in children and adults.

National Association for Gifted Children (NAGC)
1155 15th Street NW, Suite 1002
Washington, DC 20005

The association publishes a journal and a newsletter, as well as other material in gifted education. NAGC also conducts an annual convention. The association is active in promoting legislation. Membership is composed of progressional and parents.

National/State Leadership Training Institute on the Gifted and Talented
316 West Second Street, Suite PH-C
Los Angeles, CA 90012

This group provides workshops and consultation for parents, educators, and administrators of the gifted. In addition, they publish many books and other printed materials.

Supporting Emotional Needs of Gifted (SENG)
School of Professional Psychology
Wright State University
P.O. Box 2745
Dayton, OH 45401

This association is dedicated to meeting the emotional and social needs of the gifted. A variety of services are offered, including an annual conference.

The World Council for Gifted and Talented Children, Inc.
Executive Secretary
College of Education
Lemar University
Beaumont, TX 77704

This association promotes the needs of the gifted and creative worldwide. An international conference is conducted every two years.

• • •

Appendix C

Journals in Gifted Education

G/C/T
350 Weinacker Avenue
Mobile, AL 36604

This magazine serves as a resource to parents, teachers and other professionals interested in gifted and creative youth. It is published five times per year.

Gifted Child Quarterly
1155 15th Street NW #1002
Washington, DC 20005

This journal focuses on research, program description and evaluation, and other topics of interest in the field of gifted education. It is published by the National Association for Gifted Children.

Journal of Creative Behavior
Creative Educational Foundations, Inc.
State University College
1300 Elmwood Avenue
Buffalo, NY 14222

The focus of this journal is primarily research and program practices in the area of creative behavior in children and adults.

Journal for the Education of the Gifted
1920 Association Drive
Reston, VA 22091

Articles on programs, research, and other related topics in gifted education appear in this publication. It is the official journal of The Association for the Gifted.

Roeper Review
Roeper City and County Schools
2190 North Woodward
Bloomfield Hills, WI 48013

Theme issues are frequently published in this journal. Although research articles are published along with program descriptions, practical applications are given.

Appendix D

Model Constitution
Any Town Association for Gifted
and Talented Education

Model Constitution

ARTICLE I. Name

This shall be a nonprofit organization and shall be called Any Town Association for Gifted and Talented Education.

ARTICLE II. Purposes

The purposes of the association shall be:

1. To provide a forum for the development of public awareness of the needs of the gifted and talented;
2. To serve as an interchange of information on the subject of gifted and talented;
3. To develop cooperation with community and professional organizations;
4. To provide an organized "voice" for parents, teachers, administrators, school board members and others concerned with unmet needs of the gifted and talented.

ARTICLE III. Membership

Membership in the Association shall be open to all persons interested in the purposes of the Association upon payment of dues as provided herein. A member in good standing is a member whose dues for the current year are paid or have been waived by the Executive Board.

ARTICLE IV. Dues

Dues shall be payable annually in October for the ensuing year. The dues shall be in an amount set by the Executive Board and approved by the membership at regular meetings. In the event the amount set by the Executive Board for any year is not approved, the dues shall be the same amount as those last approved by the membership.

ARTICLE V. Annual Meeting

The regular meeting in April shall be known as the annual meeting and shall be for the purpose of electing officers, receiving reports of officers and committees, and for any other business that may arise.

ARTICLE VI. Officers

The officers of this Association shall be President, Vice President, Secretary and Treasurer. Said officers shall be elected at the time of the annual meeting. Prior to the annual meeting, a special committee shall be appointed by the Executive Board for the purpose of seeking a qualified person or persons who shall be suitable for the said officers and whose names it shall submit to the membership.

Duties of the Officers

1. The President shall:
    a. preside at all meetings of the Association and at all Executive Board meetings,
    b. be ex-officio member of all committees, except the nominating committee referred to in Article X herein,
    c. appoint the chair of all committees, both standing and special,
    d. remove committee chairs with the consent of the Executive Board,
    e. perform all the other duties pertaining to the office, and entrusted by the membership, in order that the

objectives and purposes of this Association be fulfilled.

2. The Vice President shall:
   a. assume the duties of the President, in the absence of or at the request of the President,
   b. schedule programs for the year,
   c. perform those functions which the President shall direct.

3. The Treasurer shall:
   a. receive and deposit all monies of the Council,
   b. disburse such sums as provided by the budget or as voted by the Executive Board,
   c. keep an accurate record of receipts and expenditures,
   d. present a brief financial statement at every regular meeting of the membership and also at Executive Board meetings if requested,
   e. make a detailed financial report as directed by the President,
   f. perform all other functions as directed by the President.

ARTICLE VII.   Executive Board

1. Duties
   a. Except as otherwise provided in this Constitution, the Executive Board shall have the power to transact the business of the Association.
   b. The Executive Board shall consist of the President, the Vice President, the Secretary, and Treasurer, and standing committee chairpersons.
   c. Each officer and committee chairperson shall have one vote on any one issue.
   d. There shall be no voting by proxy.
   e. No business of the Executive Board shall be conducted unless a quorum is present.
   f. In no case shall any one member have more than one vote on any one issue.

g. Budget
   (1) The Executive Board shall present to the membership for its approval an annual budget for the period October 1 through September 30. This budget shall be presented by the October meeting and approved at that time.
   (2) In the event the budget is not approved at this meeting, the Executive Board shall proceed forthwith to present an acceptable budget.
h. In the event that a committee chairperson has been absent for three consecutive Executive Board meetings, the President shall, with the approval of the Executive Board, replace her/him with another chairperson.
i. The Executive Board shall meet every month unless otherwise voted by the Board.
j. The Executive Board shall arrange for an annual audit of the books of the Treasurer.

ARTICLE VIII.   Standing Committees

1. The standing committees may be provided herein or as otherwise directed by the Executive Board.

Legislative Action	Program
Newsletter	Scholarship

2. The chair of standing committees shall present general plans of work to the Executive Board for approval. No action shall be taken until the general plans are approved. Upon approval of such plans, the committee shall take charge of and execute them. The committee shall execute other instructions that may be given it by the Executive Board.

ARTICLE IX.   Meetings

1. Dates
   a. Regular meetings of this Association shall be held monthly, unless otherwise provided by the membership or the Executive Board.

b. In the event a meeting date is changed, at least five days notice of said meeting dates must be given the membership.

ARTICLE X. Elections and Terms of Office

1. Nominations
   a. Nominating Committee: A nominating committee of three members shall be appointed annually in February by the Executive Board. The nominating committee shall prepare a slate of officers to be presented at the regular meeting of the Executive Board prior to the annual meeting and at the annual meeting.
   b. Nominations will be accepted from the floor at both of these meetings.
   c. The Secretary shall notify the membership of the slate of proposed officers before the regular meeting prior to the annual meeting.
   d. Members of the nominating committee may be nominated for the offices.

2. All officers shall serve for one year from annual meeting to annual meeting and until their successors shall have been elected and appointed. They may be reelected to serve consecutive terms.

ARTICLES XI. Vacancies in Office

1. In the event that a vacancy arises in any office other than that of the President, the vacancy shall be filled by the Executive Board.

2. In the event of a vacancy in the office of the President, the Vice President shall succeed and assume the office until a new President is appointed by the Executive Board.

ARTICLE XII. Amendments

1. This Constitution and By-laws may be amended by a majority vote of membership present at the monthly meeting.

2. When a motion to amend is properly before the membership, it shall be the duty of the Secretary to provide the notice in writing to the members.

3. In order to properly place a motion to amend this Constitution before the membership, the following steps may be taken:
   a. A motion must be approved and seconded.
   b. This motion must be approved by majority vote.
   c. This motion must be presented in writing to the secretary.
   d. This motion shall then be tabled until the next regular meeting or until a special meeting for its consideration shall be called. At this meeting, proper notice having been given, it shall be read, discussed and voted upon.

ARTICLE XIII.   Rules of Order

Roberts' Rules of Order, as most recently revised, shall be the authority for procedures in all cases in which they are applicable, and in which they are not inconsistent with these Bylaws.

● ● ●

SAMPLE NEWS RELEASE

News Release

DATE:

FROM:

> Your Organization
> Street Address
> City, State, Zip Code

FOR FURTHER INFORMATION:

> Organization Contact Name
> Telephone Number

For Immediate Release

Type text here and be sure to include: who, what, when, where, why. If there is a charge for attending, mention it.

NOTE: Send your release to all daily and weekly newspapers in your area addressed to "Community Events" or similar title. Record-keeping can be very time-effective. Many groups keep records on previous news releases (and copies), future publication possibilities, city editors, education editors, lists of local and regional newspapers. Many keep historical accounts of speakers and their topics, as well as newsletters disseminated by the group for later references.

● ● ●

SAMPLE
PUBLIC SERVICE ANNOUNCEMENT

Public Service Announcement

DATE:

FROM:

    Your Organization
    Street Address
    City, State, Zip Code

FOR FURTHER INFORMATION:

    Organization Contact Name
    Telephone Number

TIME: 30 seconds

For Immediate Release

Type text here and be sure to include: Who, what, when, where, why. Mention if there is a charge for attending.

NOTE: Federal regulations require radio and television stations to provide a certain percentage of time to public and nonprofit agencies and organizations. Cable news and weather stations can also be most helpful in providing air time for public service announcements.

Keep a list of contact people such as TV producers, news staff, and writers.

• • •

SAMPLE
Parent Group Evaluation Form

Do the time/place/dates of our meetings fit into your schedule?

Is meeting notification communicated to you in a timely and effective manner?

What topics/speakers would you suggest for consideration for upcoming programs?

Do you feel the needs and goals of the group are being met?

What suggestions do you have for increased participation?

In what ways could children be more directly involved with the group?

Do you have any suggestions for community service projects for the group?

Please comment on ways in which you feel the group could be improved.

● ● ●

Appendix E

Bridging the Gap: Guidelines for Parents and Teachers *

Bridging the Gap:
Guidelines for Parents and Teachers

1. Recognize that home and school have different goals,
    tasks, situations, and constraints. Schools focus primar-
    ily on academic preparation, secondarily on socializa-
    tion. At home, the focus is primarily on socialization,
    secondarily on academics.

2. Both are very important in the long-term effects on
    gifted children, though of the two, homes may be more
    crucial. The ideal is for both to work together, to avoid
    conflicts or to bridge gaps.

3. Misunderstandings, differences in expectations, and dis-
    appointments usually can be avoided if parents become
    involved in the school functions early and continually.
    Parents, making yourself known to teachers, principals,
    guidance counselors, etc. early and frequently is impor-
    tant.

---

*Reprinted by permission. Information provided by:
    James T. Webb, Ph.D.
    Supporting the Emotional Needs of Gifted
    Wright State University
    School of Professional Psychology
    P.O. Box 1102
    Dayton, OH 45401

4. Parents should offer to help teachers, librarians, etc. in ways that benefit *all* children, not just "gifted" students. Avoid appearing elitist. Gifted children's educational needs are often different, but gifted children are not necessarily "better."

5. Support school efforts to plan for able children. Help to interest the PTA and the school administration/school board in the topic. Support study groups on gifted children and similar cooperative endeavors. Ask if parents can attend school in-service programs on gifted children.

6. Parents — make periodic gifts of books, articles or tapes about gifted children to the teacher, principal, guidance counselor or librarian.

7. Parents and teachers must not give the impression of "pushing" or "exhibiting" a child, but should continually strive to give the child whatever he or she needs to reach his or her potential.

8. Teachers most often fear/expect that parents of gifted children will be "unguided missiles" and critically demanding of special favors for their child. Parents most often fear/expect that teachers will not understand and will "take it out" on their child. Rarely is either one true.

9. Teachers increasingly are more informed about gifted children and their special educational needs, but also are often hampered, themselves, by the constraints of the educational system within which they work and their responsibilities to the other children they teach. The search for solutions to school problems must start with the realities of the classroom, in the same way that solutions to home problems must start with the realities there.

10. If a problem seems to exist between home and school, first consider that what the child tells you is that child's

perception. The problem may be with the perception, rather than with the situation.

11. Parent-teacher consultations are strongly recommended. Not only do they allow sharing of information, and avoidance of being manipulated by the child, but also promote building of a focused alliance to stimulate the child's achievement and self-concept.

12. Define concretely for yourself what you hope to accomplish in the parent-teacher meeting(s), and begin to formulate a specific plan for achieving those goals in the meeting(s).

13. Prior to your conference, evaluate what *new* information you have, and consider how your information might differ from what the other knows about the child. Seek to *share* observations and information.

14. How much of your information can the other use constructively? Will your information:
    • Demonstrate a pattern, or promote understanding, or evoke compassion?
    • Frighten the other, lead to unhelpful behavior, or disrupt the relationship with the child?

15. Express understanding of the other's feelings and viewpoints in the situation. Attempt to engage the other as an ally rather than as an enemy. Be sensitive to the other possibly feeling invaded.

16. Avoid blaming. Recognize that most persons do not act out of malice, but rather they drift into problem situations through oversight, lack of information, or attempting to handle too many responsibilities. Only rarely is there a teacher or parent who "just doesn't care" or who is actively malicious.

17. Avoid trying to bludgeon insight or your point of view into others. It does not work, and only results in resentment and hardening of positions.

18. Initially ask for the other's overall perceptions of the child — how the child is doing and what the teacher's or parent's plans are. This allows you to learn where you are starting from — and may bring some pleasant surprises.

19. Parents — give the teacher professional respect in your approach, even if you must disagree at times. Teachers need support also. It is important that you not appear to be attacking the teacher's ability or character.

20. Teachers — parents need to feel genuinely listened to and respected, rather than like intruders or "only a parent." They are only seeking what is best for their child — from their point of view.

21. In your conversations, avoid saying "What are *you* going to do about . . ." Instead say, "What can *we* do about . . ."

22. In sharing new information, start with those parts most likely to fit with the other's perceptions, and which will tend to build a common base from which to begin. Actively seek the other's opinions. Ask what the other thinks about each new piece of information.

23. Gradually share more information as the conversation progresses. Avoid "dumping" all of your complaints or new/different information onto the other. Instead, after each major piece of information, stop to check to see how this fits with the other's perceptions or beliefs about the child or the situation.

24. Receive new information from the other as openly as possible, and ask questions in a spirit of curiosity rather than defensiveness.

25. When making a point, give examples and data rather than just general opinions.

26. If you have data from an "outside expert," remember that this can often be quite threatening since it tends to imply "see, you are wrong!" Try to present such information in ways that allow the other not to "lose face."

27. Focus on solutions or attempts at problem-solving that are in small steps, measurable in outcome, and achievable. Avoid broad sweeping generalities such as "improve self-concept."

28. Always attempt to give an alternative when making suggestions or recommendations.

29. Emphasize ways showing that working jointly is clearly preferable, and that will make teaching or parenting easier or more enjoyable.

30. Try to come to agreement on some specific joint action plan, even if it represents only a partial solution, or to meet again.

31. If agreement is not reached, or is only partially reached, do not insist on a definitive answer right then. Give the other person time to think and reflect on the new possibilities or new data.

32. Follow-up the conference with a brief letter of appreciation, and confirming your understanding of the issues, information, and actions that are planned by each.

33. Often it may be wise to involve the guidance counselor, principal or others in parent-teacher conferences, though this can leave one or more people feeling "ganged-up on." Realize that administrators must be supportive of their teachers, at least in public, but that they are typically also quite sensitive to concerns by parents and other members of the public.

34. Sometimes, though, conferences do not work. Know when to give up trying to build a bridge or to change a situation. Instead, the focus may have to be on coaching the child to cope, building a safety net, or moving the child to a new class or new school.

35. Most of all, keep on modeling active problem-solving for the child!

• • •